D1567488

Tempt Me

Tempt Me

The Fine Art
of Minnesota Cooking

KATHRYN STRAND KOUTSKY
LINDA KOUTSKY

MINNESOTA
HISTORICAL
SOCIETY PRESS

This publication is partially funded by a grant from Furthermore,
a program of the J. M. Kaplan Fund.

Credits for cover and front matter illustrations:
COVER: Farmer Seed and Nursery Co. apples, Anderson Horticultural Library; *New Party Cakes for All Occasions*; *Sunday Magazine*, Hennepin History Museum; *Treasured Polish Recipes for Americans*; *Cake Baking Made Easy with Airy Fairy*; Minnegasco's *Festive Foods*. BACK COVER: Gold Medal Flour recipe card. ENDSHEETS: *Just Right Cookbook* from the Dairy Council of the Twin Cities. PAGE I: *The Farmer Country Kitchen Cook Book*. PAGES II–III: *The Pillsbusy Cook-Book*. PAGE V: Pillsbury's *A Little Book for a Little Cook*. PAGE VI: Blue Earth City Rollermills, Steve Ketcham. PAGE VII: *Creamette's Encore Cookbook*. PAGE 1: *The Pillsbusy Cook-Book*.

www.mnhspress.org

The Minnesota Historical Society Press is a member of
the Association of American University Presses.
Manufactured in China
10 9 8 7 6 5 4 3 2 1

∞ The paper used in this publication meets the minimum requirements of the American National Standard for Information Sciences—Permanence for Printed Library Materials, ANSI Z39.48-1984.

International Standard Book Number
ISBN: 978-0-87351-997-7 (cloth)

Library of Congress Cataloging-in-Publication Data available upon request.

This book would never have made it to the printer without the help of husband and father Dean Koutsky and friend Madeline Betsch, who both read every word at least twice. A special thank-you goes to the Minnesota Historical Society Press publisher Pam McClanahan, our tireless editor Shannon Pennefeather, learned helpers Deb Miller and Patrick Coleman, and production manager extraordinaire Daniel Leary. We couldn't have celebrated Minnesota's wonderful cooking art without these generous people and many more who helped us along the way.

TABLE OF CONTENTS

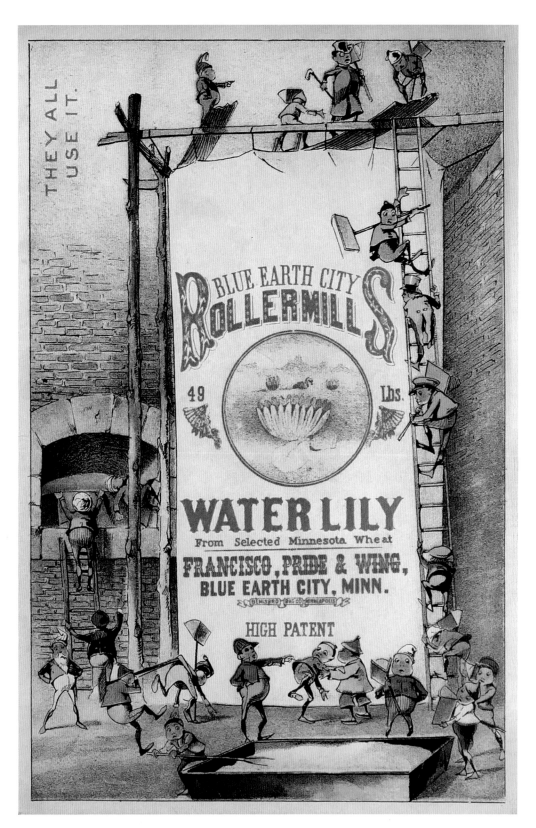

PREFACE

Kitchen planning was a big part of my interior design career, and in Minnesota there were a lot of cooks—both amateur and professional. We were, after all, in the land of big food companies, and the region also held large national advertising companies that worked for the food companies.

The booming business of food photography made use of stylists to design backgrounds for food photos, and I signed on. The jobs came fast! For ten years I provided the dishes, backgrounds, and props in hundreds of still life photos for local food companies. I designed sets for TV commercials, including lots of kitchens, and we resold the beautiful architectural antiques that we used on the sets.

I enjoyed designing those gorgeous four-color photo and film backgrounds. But I also loved the old vintage drawings, beautiful illustrations, and luminous paintings that had enlivened cookbooks and food products in the early years–before photography took over. I started collecting old cookbooks and package designs—but only the ones with fabulous art. As it happens with those of us who start collections, it grew quickly, and I soon decided that I needed to share. Surrounded by artists, cooks, and history buffs among my family and friends, I had a lot of help to sort through mounds of paper and piles of artifacts for this book. Thank you, everyone!

—KSK

Creamettes Encore Cookbook, 1970s. Table props by Kathryn Strand Koutsky, who provided the glass jars, brass scoop, and tabletop—and still uses the jars in her kitchen today.

When I was growing up, both of my parents worked in creative fields. My father was an advertising art director, and my mother selected props for ads and commercials so the locations looked lived in. She also designed our home, which had a large living room and an open kitchen and dining area that flowed into the family room—very ahead of its time in the 1970s. It became the site for many ads and commercials. My sister and I would come home from school to find the street filled with film trucks and camera crews spilling into our front yard. Models, such as Loni Anderson, would use our bedrooms as dressing rooms. On those days we'd usually head to the basement. Eventually Mom's propping business grew so big that she paid us money to rent what was our play-room. It was an interesting childhood. When my sister and I wanted regular peace and quiet after school, we headed to our grandparents' house a couple blocks away. But that energy and creativity inspired us both; my sister is the lead designer at a home remodeling company, and I design books.

As with most complicated projects, this one was accomplished with a great team. My mother Kathryn had the vision for this book several years ago, pulled the themes together, and wrote the copy. My father Dean made preliminary layout sketches to show how items could be sized or grouped on a page. We spent many, many hours together around the large dining room table with vast numbers of photos scattered about, contemplating the options and preliminary layouts. Whenever a conflict arose, a neighborhood dog we all liked would walk by on the sidewalk outside and provide comic relief. I hope you enjoy this visual feast of Minnesota's artistic bounty.

—LK

Dedicated to all the unrecognized artists
whose work enlivens food products
and cookbooks to this day.

INTRODUCTION

Pour yourself a cup of coffee and settle in to admire the fine art of Minnesota cooking. When it comes to food, "you eat with your eyes first!"

From 1880 to 1980, Minnesota food companies reached out to customers with beautiful hand-painted food illustrations. Artists ranging from the nationally famous to the regionally talented turned out stunning oil paintings, gorgeous watercolors, and delightful drawings to attract customers' attention—and it worked. Many of those companies grew to become recognized beyond the state's borders, across the country, and around the world.

Minnesota has always been a rich and bountiful land, and early industries took advantage of the state's agricultural treasures. Cookbooks and food advertising from hundreds of flour mills included extraordinary illustrations, and these images are celebrated on the pages to come. Printed pieces from vegetable, dairy, and fruit companies exhibited equally artful treatments and shared mouth-watering recipes.

Cooking art followed evolving styles of American art, from Victorian excess to modernist minimalism. Still life paintings of cakes and pies worthy of art museum display beamed from cookbook pages. Whimsical paintings leapt out from company trading cards, spice tins, and can labels. Garden catalog and seed packet images tempted gardeners to get out the hoe. Carried in the artworks are glimpses of other issues of the day for discerning readers to spot: the aspirations of the middle class, offhand racism, and the position of women.

To accompany all this art, simple recipes offer a flavor of the times. As it turns out, most of these vintage selections are surprisingly interesting to read, and they don't take all day in the kitchen. To those testing out these historical recipes, be warned: as you put on your apron, you'll also need your thinking cap, because old-time instructions are more intuitive than directive. None of the early recipes have been modified, and the measurements, ingredients, and methods vary wildly. Your ingenuity will be tested with instructions like "bake until done."

Over these one hundred years, historical events, life-changing inventions, and evolving fashions had a huge influence on American lives. As we tied together pivotal national history with creative art movements and joyful period cooking, the synergism was spellbinding. We hope you will find the pages of *Tempt Me: The Fine Art of Minnesota Cooking* surprising, enlightening, and entertaining.

Another cup of coffee?

CHAPTER 1
1880–1900

I t was called the Golden Age of Illustration, and Victorian cookbooks featured food illustrations produced in color for the first time. Initially the effect was subtle, but as printing processes evolved, the many and various shades soon reached vibrant and dramatic levels. Bakers and cooks responded to beautiful food illustrations, and demand for painters and illustrators soared.

The American economy was also growing rapidly. With the introduction of electricity, telephones, radios, zippers, and bottle caps, great social change was evident. Small farms became bigger farms, and villages grew into large cities. Railroads brought in a bounty of new food products, and families traveled out to experience new parts of the country. Mark Twain penned *Adventures of Huckleberry Finn*, the first Great American Novel. Life was getting more interesting.

Minnesota's milling companies and vegetable and fruit growers featured cookbooks with increasingly alluring illustrations. Cookbook art reflected down-home appeal, with kitchen windows overlooking pastoral fields of bountiful grain. Area seed growers published awe-inspiring paintings of produce that are collected and reprinted even today. Food companies' advertising drew on the talents of nationally famous artists who joined an impressive list of Minnesota painters.

Those who gathered around wood-fired cookstoves found appealing meals as recipes made use of what was plentiful from nearby farms. But cooking instructions often left room for interpretation. Ingredients might include butter the size of an egg or spice to cover a three-cent piece, gauging oven temperatures required years of experience, and cooking times were a calculated guess.

But kitchen work was becoming easier at the turn of the century. The Gilded Age would soon progress into a new era, bringing an entirely different world—and fresh perspectives when it came to food and art.

Minnesota's First Cookbooks

Early American cookbooks had few illustrations, just page after page of text. It was not only hard to be a cook; it was visually boring.

Many of Minnesota's first cookbooks were published by local merchants who knew that giving out free cookbooks would attract buyers into their shops. Small manufacturers easily placed their product catalogs in homes if the title featured the word "cookbook."

T. K. Gray's 1893 drugstore was located in the heart of Minneapolis on Bridge Square by the new Hennepin Avenue bridge. His cookbook held ads for floor paint, dyes, pain eradicators, and animal feed. The store did not sell food, but the offer of a free cookbook brought in local homemakers and rural farmwives who were seeking new recipes and healthful remedies for their families.

The cover's fancy leaves, vines, ribbons, and scrolls provided an artful background to hand-drawn lettering.

SQUASH PIE

A generous half pint of stewed and sifted squash, one egg, one piece of butter the size of an egg, one-half cup of sugar, one-half pint of sweet milk, one-half teaspoonful each of nutmeg and cinnamon, and a pinch of salt; beat all together but the milk, add that. Bake in a deep pie dish three-fourths of an hour.

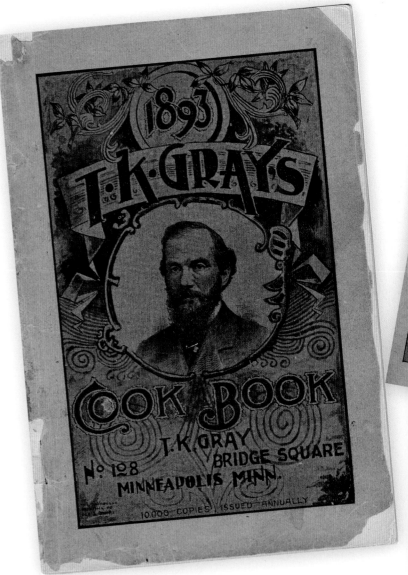

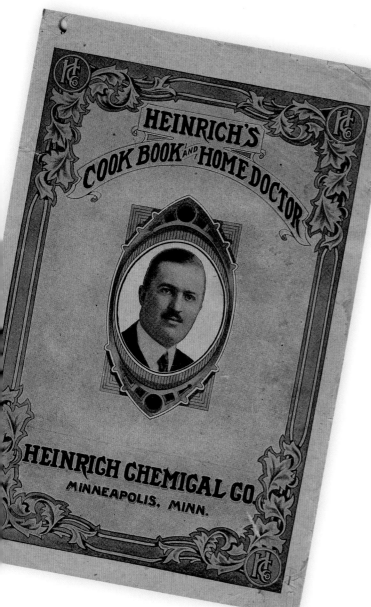

Health was uppermost in the minds of early Minnesotans, and companies offered cookbooks as enticements for people to leaf through their catalogs of early medical products. Popular recipes were cleverly placed among the bottles of home remedies for sale throughout the pages.

Heinrich's book boasted classic corner embellishments of swirling acanthus leaves and Roman capital type that was thought to command attention and respect. The strong ornamentation hinted that there was more to look at between the covers.

Promoting fine art, Heinrich offered color reproductions of American paintings to hang on the parlor wall. A copy of portrait artist Francis M. Day's oil painting of mother, daughter, and baby boy could be ordered for twenty-five cents, postpaid. Buyers would have been pleased by the color reproduction of the beautiful painting that arrived in the mail, even with the Heinrich ad at the bottom.

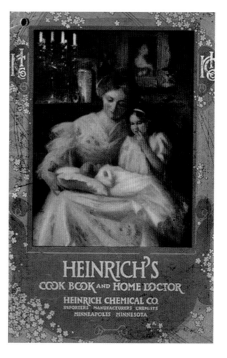

EGGS À LA SUISSE

Take a shallow baking dish and put two large tablespoonfuls of butter in a little milk, then a layer of grated cheese. Break a number of eggs carefully and put them in the dish, being careful to keep them separate. Season with salt and pepper, sprinkle cheese over the top, and put in the oven. As soon as the cheese is brown, they are ready to serve.

Engravings go back as far as the Middle Ages and for centuries were the best way to reproduce an image. Engraving artists incised detailed line work on copper or metal plates. Ink was applied in the grooves, paper was pressed on top, and a beautiful image emerged. It was the perfect way to illustrate food and cooking products.

ONION PIE

| 2 cups crushed soda crackers |
| 6 tablespoons butter, softened |
| 3 cups onions, sliced |
| 3 tablespoons butter |
| 3 eggs, beaten |
| 1 cup milk |
| 1 1/2 teaspoons salt |
| 1 teaspoon freshly cracked pepper |
| 2 cups mild cheddar cheese, shredded |

Combine soda crackers and softened butter; press into a 10-inch pie plate. Sauté onions in remaining butter until transparent. Spoon into crust. Combine eggs, milk, salt, pepper, and cheese. Pour over onions. Bake at medium heat for 30 to 35 minutes.

PASTRY & PIES

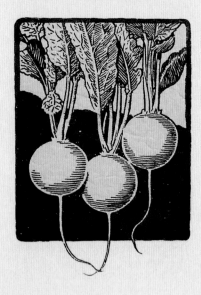

EXTRA EARLY BARLETTA. BEST FOR PICKLING.

Made in Minneapolis by Northwest Stove Works, this cookstove was featured in an exquisitely detailed engraving showing curved brackets, open latticework, and Eastlake-style linear ornamentation—all cast in iron. Cooking on a cast-iron stove required muscles—to open the oven door, lift the burner covers, and ladle water out of the hot-water tank. Then there was the job of bringing in logs or coal and taking out the ashes. Maintaining oven temperatures required a guess and a prayer. Still, many good cooks figured out a system that delivered consistent results.

Flour amounts were determined by how the dough felt when all the ingredients had been put together; baking temperatures depended on local weather conditions—even for Washburn-Crosby's famous bread flour.

YEAST BREAD NO. 1 – FOR TWO LOAVES

Two quarts of flour, half a cupful of yeast, nearly a pint and a half of water, half a tablespoonful each of lard, sugar, and salt. Sift the flour into a bread pan, and, after taking out a cupful for use in kneading, add the salt, sugar, yeast, and the water, which must be about blood warm (or, say, one hundred degrees if cold weather, and about eighty in the hot season). Beat well with a strong spoon. When well mixed, sprinkle a little flour on the board, turn out the dough on this, and knead from twenty to thirty minutes. Put back in the pan. Hold the lard in the hand long enough to have it very soft. Rub it over the dough. Cover closely, that neither dust nor air can get in, and set in a warm place. It will rise in eight or nine hours. In the morning shape into loaves. Let rise an hour where the temperature is between ninety and one hundred degrees. Bake in an oven that will brown a teaspoonful of flour in five minutes, from forty-five to sixty minutes.

Washburn-Crosby Company

Published by the Washburn-Crosby Company flour mills of Minneapolis in 1880, *Miss Parloa's New Cook Book* was one of the first cookbooks printed with color on the cover and was an immediate success with cooks all over the country.

Cadwallader and William Washburn founded the Minneapolis Milling Company in 1856, and John Crosby joined them in 1877. The successful Washburn-Crosby Company would become General Mills in 1928. Public tours were promoted in engravings of the up-to-date mills.

The new art form on the cookbook cover was subtle because color printing was in its early stages. Still, the image of a dining table filled with fancy food delivered by a maid appealed to those who dreamed of fine in-home dining.

Following recipes in the late 1800s was not easy as directions and amounts were not yet standardized. Large amounts called for coffee cups, teacups, or wineglasses found in the cupboard; smaller amounts were measured by everyday spoons from the kitchen drawer: large, medium, and small. Recipes were written in paragraph form, ingredients were not always listed in order, and methods were not spelled out.

FEDERAL CAKE

One pint of sugar, one and a half cupfuls of butter, three pints of flour, four eggs, two wineglasses of milk, two of wine, two of brandy, one teaspoonful of cream of tartar, half a teaspoonful of saleratus, fruit and spice to taste. Bake in deep pans, the time depending on the quantity of fruit used.

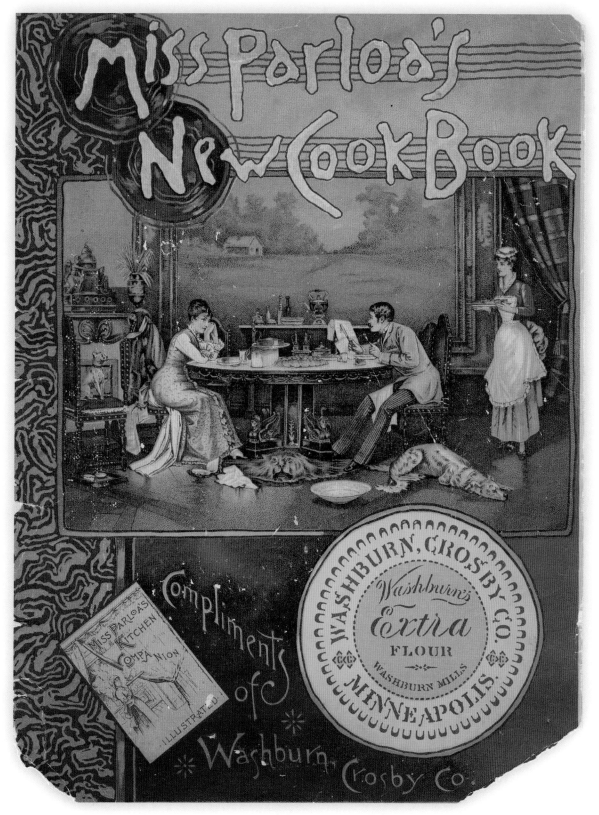

Miss Parloa's New Cook Book

Compliments of Washburn, Crosby Co.

MISS PARLOA'S KITCHEN COMPANION
ILLUSTRATED

WASHBURN, CROSBY & CO.
Washburn's Extra FLOUR
WASHBURN MILLS
MINNEAPOLIS.

The Golden Age of Illustration

The late 1800s were the dawn of the Golden Age of Illustration. Independent mills in Minnesota proudly promoted themselves with some of the most amazing art ever painted for the milling industry. Advertising artwork for flour looked like it belonged in a museum. In the decades that followed, local flour was featured prominently in cookbooks from hundreds of mills located throughout the state.

At the time, Minnesota was the center of the world for flour production, and the state held its position as the largest flour producer in the nation for more than fifty years.

A poster for the Gardner Mill featured the Hague school style of painting that relied on romantic country scenes in bold colors. The Dutch artistry reflected the background of some of the settlers in the Hastings area.

SKILLET BISCUIT BREAD

2 cups all-purpose flour

1 1/2 teaspoons sugar

1 tablespoon baking powder

1 teaspoon salt

8 tablespoons cold butter, cubed

3/4 cup buttermilk

In a large bowl, combine flour, sugar, baking powder, and salt. Cut butter into mixture until it begins to look shaggy. Make a well in the flour mixture and slowly add milk. Knead dough with fingers and add more milk if necessary. On a lightly floured board, pat out dough to fit a 10-inch cast-iron skillet. Butter bottom and sides of skillet; place dough in pan. Bake in a hot oven for 12 minutes or until golden brown. Serve with butter, honey, and jam.

Swirls of the American flag and gracefully flowing gowns wrapped Victorian ladies in dramatic flair as they contemplated waving fields of grain. Paintings in the classic Romantic style stressed ideas of art that included strong emotion and creative imagination. These mills accomplished their idealistic ambitions of selling flour with impressive elegance.

Color Comes to Cooking

"BEST in the WORLD". All Grocers handle it.

Daily Capacity 13.500 Barrels...

Minnesota companies began to use new color lithography to expand awareness of their products with premiums, mailings, recipe cards, and cookbooks. This printing style was an illustrator's dream. All the hues of the rainbow were available, reproduction was clear, fine details held firm, and colors didn't run. Bakers and cooks adored the fun, imaginative, and colorful publications that would enliven their kitchens.

Pillsbury's BEST XXXX Minneapolis, Minn.

Is the best.

This Flour always on top.

WASHBURN, CROSBY CO

MINNEAPOLIS, MINN. U.S.A.

MERCHANT MILLERS.

CHICKEN CURRY

One chicken, weighing three pounds; three-fourths of a cupful of butter, two large onions, one heaping tablespoonful of curry powder, three tomatoes or one cupful of the canned article, enough cayenne to cover a silver three-cent piece, salt, one cupful of milk. Put the butter and onions, cut fine, on to cook. Stir all the while until brown; then put in the chicken, which has been cut in small pieces, the curry, tomatoes, salt, and pepper. Stir well. Cover tightly, and let simmer one hour, stirring occasionally; then add the milk. Boil up once, and serve with boiled rice. This makes a very rich and hot curry, but, for the real lover of the dish, none too much so.

Ceresota Flour

Northwestern Consolidated Milling Company was once the second-largest milling company in Minneapolis and operated about a quarter of the independent mills in the late 1890s. Ceresota was the name of its flour.

As the sun set outside a curtained window, it was time to set out the bread and rolls for dinner. But for dessert, Ceresota cookbook designers chose delicate watercolor illustrations in pastel colors with creamy, rich shadings that would make readers want to eat dessert first.

MAPLE MOUSSE

3/4 cup maple syrup

1/4 cup cane syrup (or equal parts corn syrup and honey)

3 eggs, separated

2 cups cream

Heat syrups and pour over beaten yolks of eggs, stirring briskly. Whip the cream and the whites of the eggs, and fold into the first mixture. Pack in ice and salt and let stand several hours without stirring.

JELLY SHERBET

MAPLE MOUSSE

NEAPOLITAN ICE CREAM

CAFÉ FRAPPÉ

PIE CRUST

LEMON PIE

SHORT CAKE

CUP CUSTARD

THREE-MINUTE PASTE

2 cups Ceresota flour

1/2 teaspoon salt

1 egg yolk

1 teaspoon lemon juice

ice-cold water

1/2 cup butter or lard or mixture of the two

Sift the flour and salt; beat the egg and add the lemon juice and a little ice-cold water. Place the butter in a slightly warmed bowl and beat till creamy. Add the flour, mix it in lightly with a knife, and make to a light, firm dough with the egg, lemon juice, and water. Turn onto a well-floured board, roll out once, and use. This is a very rich, light paste, well adapted to small tartlets, patties, and such things.

LEMON PIE

1 cup cane syrup (or equal parts corn syrup and honey)

1 cup milk

2 tablespoons cornstarch

3 eggs

rind and juice of 1 large lemon

pinch salt

prepared unbaked pie crust

Cook the cane syrup, milk, and cornstarch together in a double boiler for 15 minutes. Beat the yolks of 2 eggs and 1 whole egg slightly and stir smooth with the first mixture. Add the lemon juice and rind and the salt and cook 1 minute. Fill the unbaked crust while hot, and bake in quick oven. When cool, make meringue of the whites of 2 eggs and return the pie to the oven to brown.

Sleepy Eye and Queen Bee Mills

Chief Sleepy Eye lived from 1780 to 1860 by Minnesota's Sleepy Eye Lake, once called "Pretty Water by the Big Trees." A flour mill was built in the town of Sleepy Eye in 1883, later moving to Minneapolis. At the turn of the century, the milling company began sending out promotional items: cookbooks, handheld fans, match holders, letter openers, caps, linens, pillows, and even pottery. They were used in homes and offices all over the region, and Sleepy Eye Mills became known all around the country. The Dakota leader's face, casually appropriated as a mascot to sell products grown on his land, kept illustrators busy for decades.

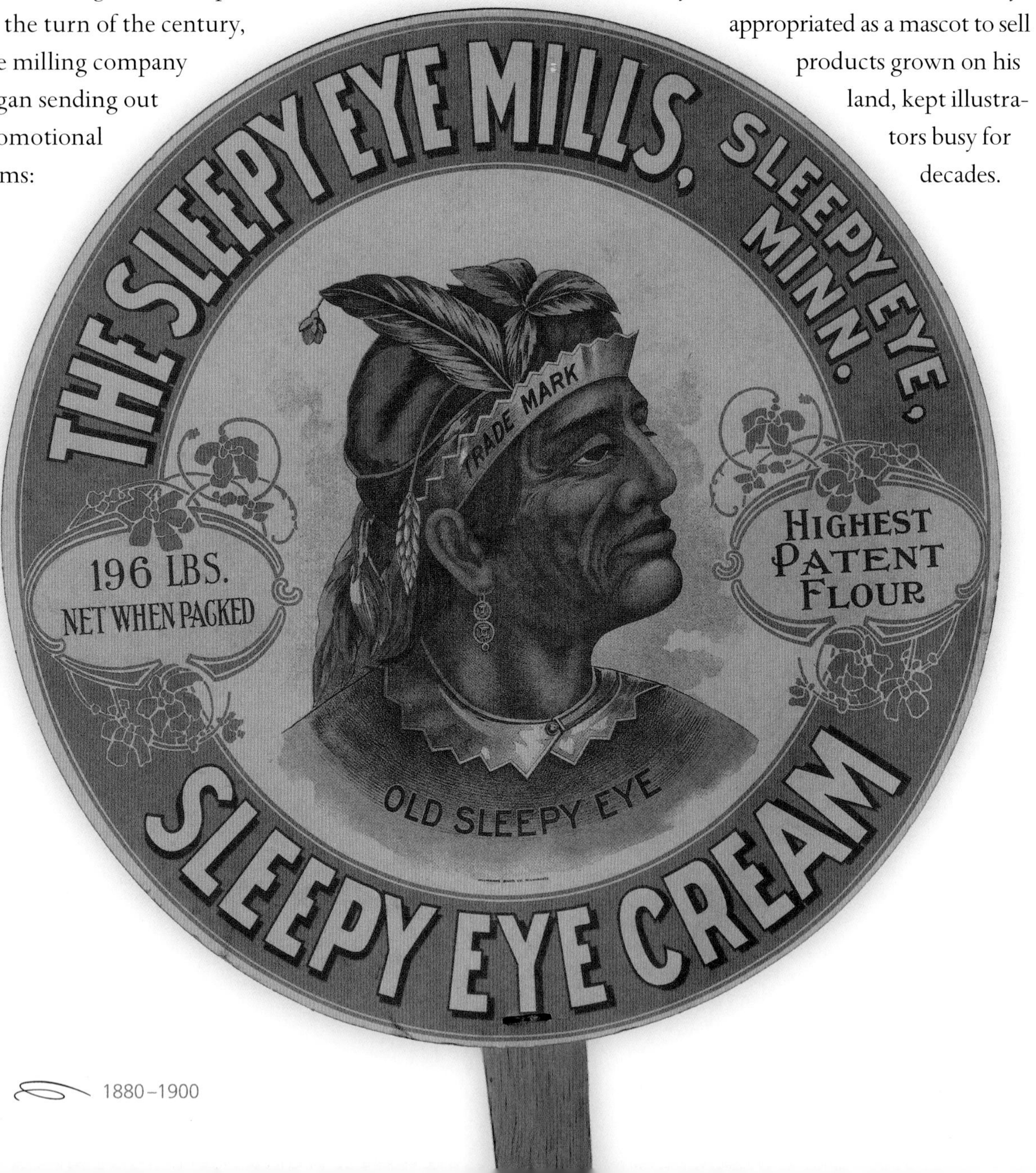

THE SLEEPY EYE MILLS, SLEEPY EYE, MINN.
TRADE MARK
196 LBS.
NET WHEN PACKED
HIGHEST PATENT FLOUR
OLD SLEEPY EYE
SLEEPY EYE CREAM

PÂTÉ DE VEAU

Three and one-half pounds finely chopped veal, one tablespoon of salt, one of pepper, two eggs, one nutmeg, three tablespoons of cream, eight of rolled crackers, butter the size of an egg; make into a loaf, put into a pan set in a little water; rub it over with butter and rolled crackers, and bake.

MOTHER'S LOVE KNOTS

One egg, one tablespoon each of sugar, butter, and milk, pinch of salt, pinch of nutmeg, Sleepy Eye cream flour to knead very hard. Roll out thin, cut like a pipe stem, tie in two or three knots, and fry in hot lard. Sprinkle with pulverized sugar while hot.

Queen Bee Flour Mills opened in Sioux Falls, Dakota Territory, in 1881, later moving its offices to Minneapolis. The illustration of pollen-filled flowers visited by a busy bee was a wise artistic choice for a logo that never needed to be updated or modernized. The charming little bee became a familiar sight in grocery stores and kitchens throughout the region.

NOODLES

Add gradually to three eggs sufficient Queen Bee flour to make a stiff batter; cut the dough in two, roll out very thin, and leave the paste on the molding board till perfectly dry. When dry, cut into narrow strips. These require about five minutes to boil and are very good to thicken soups or boiled in salt water to eat with meat dishes.

APPLE DUMPLINGS

2 cups Queen Bee flour

2 teaspoons baking powder

1/4 teaspoon salt

1/4 cup shortening

3/4 cup milk

4 apples

sugar

cinnamon or nutmeg

Sift flour, baking powder, and salt; work in shortening and mix to a dough with milk. Roll into square sheet one-third inch thick and cut into four pieces. Lay a cored and pared apple on each piece; fill the center with sugar and spice. Then draw the paste to cover the apple, make smooth, and bake on a buttered dish. When nearly baked, brush with milk, dredge with granulated sugar, and return to the oven. Serve hot.

Duluth Imperial Flour

In the 1880s, the Duluth and Superior flour mills claimed they were "the largest such operation on the planet." By 1892 the Imperial mill was considered "the most complete ever built," with crews working day and night. Wheat from the west came into the mills by rail. Barrels of flour rolled out the other side and were loaded straight-away onto Lake Superior ships, destined for ports around the world.

The fanciful hot-air balloon, suggesting breads that were light and airy, was the trademark of Duluth Imperial flour. Victorian ladies painted in brightly colored hats and corseted costumes float magically over a busy harbor. The artist's burst of creative imagination made the improbable scene fun and whimsical.

RAGGED SAILORS

2 cups Duluth Imperial flour
1/2 teaspoon salt
2 teaspoons baking powder
3 tablespoons butter
1/2 cup sugar
1/2 cup chopped nuts
2 eggs
2/3 cup milk

Sift the flour, salt, and baking powder, rub the butter in, then add sugar and nuts; mix to a soft dough with 1 egg and milk, roll out thinly, and sprinkle with sugar. Roll up with the sugar inside, cut in slices three-quarters of an inch thick, place on a greased baking tin, brush over with beaten remaining egg, and bake about 15 minutes.

PEACH COBBLER

4 cups peaches, sliced
1 cup water
1 1/2 cups sugar, divided
1 1/3 cups Duluth Imperial flour
1/4 teaspoon salt
1 1/2 teaspoons baking powder
2 eggs
1/3 cup milk

Cook the peaches, water, and 1 cup of sugar till the peaches are tender; reserve 1/2 cup of the syrup, and place the fruit and remaining syrup in a deep baking dish. Sift the flour, salt, and baking powder, add the remaining 1/2 cup of sugar, beat and add the eggs with the milk and the 1/2 cup of syrup. Mix to a smooth batter, pour over the peaches in the dish, and bake in a moderate oven 30 minutes. Serve hot.

What to Eat

From 1896 to 1900, Minneapolis publisher Pierce and Pierce provided engaging food and cooking magazines to Minnesota residents. With colors that were unusually bright and bold for the times, the illustrations caught the attention of cooks and diners immediately. *What to Eat* proclaimed that the magazine was published every month as an authority on foods, cooking, serving, table decoration, and furnishings. Also included were short stories and commentaries such as "Shakespeare and the Ethics of Eating" or "A Morning with Creole Cooks." The publication was so popular that the company moved to the larger city of Chicago. Paul Pierce went on to publish many cookbooks dedicated to the "overworked, perturbed American hostess."

Attuned to the season, the December issue included Santa serving up a holiday turkey; July featured the American flag with a Victorian lady eating ice cream under a sunshade.

SPINACH CANAPÉS

Take the leaves of about half a peck of spinach and wash thoroughly in several waters to free from sand and dirt. Drain and throw into plenty of rapidly boiling salted water and cook uncovered until done, about thirty minutes. Drain well and chop very fine. Melt a quarter of a cup of butter in a frying pan, add a heaping tablespoon of flour, stir until a light yellow, add the spinach and gradually about a pint of gravy, stock, or water. Cook until thickened and season to taste with salt and pepper. Stamp some sliced bread into rounds with a large-sized biscuit cutter. Toast and butter the bread, cover thickly with the spinach, and in the center of each place a slice of hard-boiled egg. Send to the table at once, garnished with parsley.

The activity of busy farm scenes appealed to Minnesota residents, who were mostly rural citizens in the late 1800s. Women especially appreciated the recipes and reading materials that came inside the brightly colored and sprightly illustrated magazines.

Jewell Nursery

At Lake City in the lush Mississippi River valley, gardening fan Mrs. P. A. Jewell founded the Jewell Nursery. It was 1868. About the same time, Dellon Marcus Dewey was printing pocket-sized lithograph prints of every product a plant nursery would want to sell, and by 1879 he had more than 2,300 full-color illustrations. Jewell ordered custom leather satchels to hold books filled with gorgeous fruit and plant paintings, and salesmen traveled throughout the Midwest selling their products door to door. The lavish illustrations inspired hardworking gardeners and pioneer farmers to hope for bountiful crops from Jewell plants.

OLD-FASHIONED CURRANT CREAM SCONES

2 cups all-purpose flour
1/3 cup sugar
2 teaspoons baking powder
1/2 teaspoon salt
6 tablespoons cold butter, cut into small pieces
2/3 cup fresh or dried currants
3/4 cup cold heavy cream
1 large egg

In a large bowl, mix together flour, sugar, baking powder, and salt. Cut butter into flour mixture until crumbly. Stir in currants. Whisk together cream and egg; stir into flour mixture until just combined. Place dough on a lightly floured work surface and pat into a 6-inch round. Cut into 6 wedges and transfer to a baking sheet. Place pieces together for soft edges, apart for crisp edges. Brush tops with cream and sprinkle with sugar. Bake in a hot oven until golden, 16 to 18 minutes.

Jewell's salesmen had competition from mail-order nursery catalogs with their lively illustrations and product descriptions. Soon the U.S. mail would bring catalogs directly to a customer's door and railroads would deliver the goods, spelling the end for big-book presentations and traveling plant salesmen.

Seed Catalog Covers

Rail shipping and mail order became more economical during the late 1800s. Seed and nursery companies sprouted up all over the country as seedlings became readily transportable. Catalogs were provided inexpensively to customers from coast to coast, and a new enthusiasm for backyard gardening swept the country. Covers were embellished with extraordinary drawings of big, chunky vegetables with names like Mammoth and Giant and paintings of lush fruit ripening in leafy orchards.

Consumers were the lucky recipients of some of the most beautiful still life seed catalog art ever painted.

TOMATO AND CUCUMBER SALAD

1 small red onion in bite-size pieces

2 tablespoons vinegar

3 tablespoons olive oil

1 teaspoon honey

salt and pepper

3 tomatoes, chopped

1 1/2 cucumbers in bite-size pieces

3/4 cup blue cheese, crumbled

In medium bowl, mix onion with vinegar and a little water; marinate for 15 minutes. Mix in olive oil, honey, salt, and pepper; toss in tomatoes and cucumbers. Add cheese and serve cold.

Gould's Reliable Seeds

R.L. Gould & Company
SEEDSMEN SINCE 1898
Saint Paul, Minnesota

MAY'S "FIRST OF ALL" TOMATO
THE EARLIEST TOMATO IN THE WORLD

The earliest smooth tomato of large size. Color a bright red ripening right up to the stem. It is so far superior in hardiness, suresetting of fruits, size and uniform shape that it is now planted in all sections. The plants are compact in growth, with short, close jointed branches, setting fruits very freely. The tomatoes are quite uniform in size and of smooth, regular form, they are fleshy, solid and excellent for both market and home use.

PRICE:
PKT. 10¢, 3 PKTS. 25¢, OZ. 40¢, ¼ LB. $1.00, LB. $3.00.

L. MAY & CO., ST PAUL, MINN.

THE CUMBERLAND CUCUMBER

FROM THE FIELD TO THE FACTORY.

"The wonderful new pickling variety. For description see page
Packet 10c., oz. 25c., quarter pound 60c., pound $2.00.

...UL, MINN.

To vie for attention in the competitive world of seed catalogs, artists created bright, eye-catching artworks. It all came down to which seed grower had the most beautiful cover picture, which illustration looked the most delectable. Hardworking gardeners paged through catalogs and hoped their summer vegetables would look so good.

In later years, antique seed catalog covers and vintage seed packets remained in high demand for art lovers and collectors because of their colorful and alluring original designs.

BERRY SUMMER PUDDING

1 1/4 cups sugar

3 cups fresh raspberries or strawberries

7 slices white bread, crusts removed

whipped cream

In a saucepan over medium heat, combine sugar and berries. Cook, stirring occasionally, until mixture is hot and sugar is dissolved. Cool slightly. Line a 1-quart bowl with 6 slices of bread. Pour the berry mixture over the bread and place the last slice on top. Cover mixture with butcher paper and place a weight on top of the bowl (saucers and canned goods work well) and refrigerate overnight.

To serve, invert onto a serving plate or spoon pudding from the bowl. Top with sweetened whipped cream.

BRAZILIAN. MELON FRUIT SOMETHING ALL SHOULD HAVE

FRESH FROM YOUR OWN GARDEN

SEEDS

For Garden-Farm-Lawn

Minnesota farmers grew oats right alongside their corn and wheat crops. Packages of the rolled oats were decorated with bold illustrations that would attract attention on grocery-store shelves.

Victorian moms knew that oatmeal porridge for breakfast was a healthy start to the morning and oatmeal cookies the best nighttime snack.

COUNTRY PORRIDGE

1/2 cup rolled oats

2 tablespoons real maple syrup

1 teaspoon butter

1 teaspoon cinnamon

Cook oatmeal according to package directions. Stir in maple syrup and butter. Finish with a dash of cinnamon.

HONEY OATMEAL BEDTIME COOKIES

1/2 cup butter, softened	1 cup flour
1/2 cup sugar	1/4 teaspoon salt
1/2 cup honey	1 teaspoon ground cinnamon
1 large egg	1/2 teaspoon baking soda
1 1/2 teaspoons vanilla	1 cup raisins
1 1/2 cups rolled oats	

In medium bowl, beat butter with sugar until thoroughly blended. Blend in honey. Mix in egg and vanilla until smooth. In separate bowl, mix together oats, flour, salt, cinnamon, and baking soda; blend into honey mixture. Stir in raisins. Drop dough by tablespoon onto greased baking sheet. Bake at 350°F for 12 to 14 minutes until golden brown.

For early-morning sleepyheads, bright and cheery breakfast box art offered amusement and a smile: no tabletop conversation required.

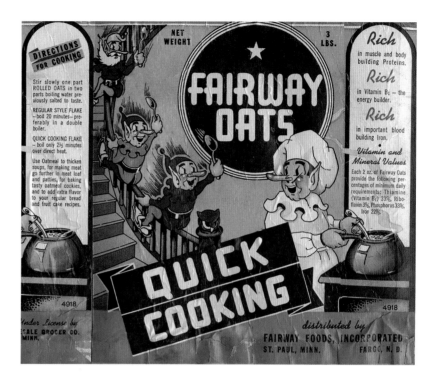

If rolled oats for breakfast didn't cut it, pancakes would get the morning off to a good start.

Cream of Wheat Company

In the 1890s, North Dakota flour miller Tom Amidon produced a breakfast porridge his family requested often at home. He named it "Cream of Wheat" after the same source of flour of the highest grade.

Amidon packed up samples of his cereal and included it in a shipment of his company's flour to the firm's New York brokers. Twelve hours after its arrival, the brokers telegraphed: "Never mind shipping us any more of your flour, but send a carload of 'Cream of Wheat.'"

By 1897, demand for Cream of Wheat had outgrown the capacity of the small Grand Forks mill, and the business moved to Minneapolis.

For the early packaging, Emery Mapes, a former printer working at the North Dakota mill, found an illustration of a black chef holding a saucepan over his shoulder. This image, which played on stereotypes of blacks as servants, was the beginning of the company's famous trademark and the launch of many legendary advertising campaigns.

GRANDMA'S CAKE

| 1 cup butter, softened |
| 2 cups sugar, divided |
| 6 eggs |
| 1 teaspoon vanilla |
| 1 cup flour |
| 1 cup uncooked Cream of Wheat cereal |
| 2 teaspoons baking powder |
| 1 cup water |

Beat butter and 1 cup of the sugar in large bowl with electric mixer until light and fluffy. Blend in eggs and vanilla. Add flour, cereal, and baking powder; mix well. Pour into lightly greased 9x13–inch baking pan. Bake on medium heat 30 to 35 minutes or until toothpick inserted in center comes out clean. Meanwhile, mix remaining 1 cup sugar and water in small saucepan. Bring to a boil on medium-high heat. Boil 5 minutes. Remove cake from oven. Immediately pour hot sugar mixture over cake. Cool cake in pan on wire rack.

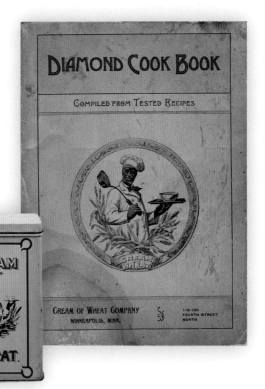

Edward Brewer of St. Paul illustrated many ads for Cream of Wheat that featured sentimental scenes of daily life. Similar to Norman Rockwell's style, his pictures of everyday family activities were often humorous and entertaining. Brewer, the son of a well-known portrait painter, was a talented muralist and portrait painter himself. Several of his paintings are in public and private collections, including at the Minnesota Historical Society and the state capitol in St. Paul.

Cream of Wheat Company

Cream of Wheat commissioned many famous American artists. National advertising featured pictures by renowned illustrator N. C. Wyeth as well as many prominent regional artists. This enterprising decision resulted in beautiful four-color prints that portrayed endearing scenes of American life. Richly colored full-page advertisements appeared monthly in dozens of national magazines. The beautiful art and collectible ads remain outstanding examples of the Golden Age of Illustration to this day.

CHOCOLATE BLANCMANGE

To one pint of fresh milk add four tablespoonfuls of chocolate and sweeten to taste. Heat to boiling point, then add very slowly one-half cup of Cream of Wheat and a pinch of salt, stirring until it thickens. Then pour into a mold. Serve with whipped cream or a light sauce.

BAKED RASPBERRY PUDDING

Take one quart of milk, one teaspoonful of salt, one cup of sugar, and two well-beaten eggs. Heat this and then pour in slowly one cup of Cream of Wheat, stirring constantly. Boil fifteen minutes; then butter a deep pudding dish and put in a layer of raspberry jam on the bottom, over which pour a layer of above, alternating until all the ingredients have been used. Bake ten minutes in a quick oven. Serve with whipped cream flavored with sherry wine.

In 1906, N. C. Wyeth wrote to his mother:

> Mr. Mapes of the Cream of Wheat telegraphed for me to run up and see him at the Waldorf Astoria. I have just completed two pictures for him $250 each, which he is immensely pleased with.

The Bronco Buster and *Where the Mail Goes Cream of Wheat Goes* are part of the Minneapolis Institute of Art's collections.

WHERE THE MAIL GOES CREAM OF WHEAT GOES

Northrup King

Northrup King was founded in 1884 as Northrup, Braslan and Company; Goodwin was added to the name in 1887, and Colonel William S. King joined the group in 1894. The long-lasting merger, known as Northrup, King and Co., became a national provider of hardy northern seeds.

Believing that seeds grown in the north were more resilient and that Minneapolis was an ideal distribution center, the owners of Northrup, King and Co. located the main building where the Great Northern and Northern Pacific Railroads came together.

RADISH COLESLAW

4 cups cabbage, shredded

2 teaspoons salt

1/2 cup sugar

1 1/2 cups carrot, shredded

5 radishes, shredded

1 cup mayonnaise

1 tablespoon vinegar

Sprinkle cabbage with salt and sugar. Let set for 2 hours, turning occasionally. Drain liquid from bowl. Add carrots and radishes. Add mayonnaise mixed with vinegar. Chill.

Northrup, King and Co. published its first illustrated seed catalogs in 1885. Displaying stunning full-color lithographs, the covers enticed buyers from all over the country and contributed to the company's success. Covers highlighting adventure attracted more attention than the usual bountiful fruit and vegetable pictures. The outdoor scenes, with their fine art quality of light and shade, were often displayed as art on kitchen walls.

Russell-Miller Occident Flour

John Russell helped form a North Dakota flour-milling business in the 1870s; Arthur Miller joined him in 1882. The name Occident, meaning "out of the west," was used for their quality flour since their milling operations took place at the western edge of the nation's wheat-growing territory. In 1907, Russell-Miller headquarters moved to Minneapolis.

BAKING POWDER CHEESE BISCUITS

2 cups Occident flour

1/4 cup baking powder

1/2 teaspoon salt

3 tablespoons shortening

3/4–1 cup milk

1/2 cup grated cheese

Sift dry ingredients together twice. Cut in shortening. Add milk gradually, until mixture is a soft, spongy dough. Turn onto floured board. Pat or roll lightly to half-inch thickness. Sprinkle cheese over half; fold over remaining half. Pinch edges together and roll again. Cut with biscuit cutter. Bake in a hot oven for 12 to 15 minutes.

Souvenir ink blotters would remain on desks and tables for a long time, but bakers would quickly add these rolls to their dinner menu.

Artists from every era have experimented with still life paintings of food and flowers. The sumptuous effect of shafts of light and patches of darkness resonated with luxuriantly colored Renaissance styles.

Occident artist Clarence W. Conaughy attended the Minneapolis School of Art and the New York School of Art. His works showcased the dramatic effects of still life painting: elegantly plated foods, even common dinner rolls, were enticing. Formal food arrangements signed by E. R. Kullberg show harmonious compositions of freshly made pastries and baked goods.

Minnesota Apples

Early settlers found only crab apples in Minnesota. But in 1886, after years of testing and apple breeding, Peter Gideon produced Minnesota's first hardy apple and named it after his wife, Wealthy. It remains one of the best apples for cooking to this day.

Other famous apples developed by the University of Minnesota include the Haralson and the Honeycrisp, now the Minnesota state apple.

BLUE-RIBBON APPLE PIE

pastry for 2-crust pie

1/2 cup sugar

1/4 cup firmly packed brown sugar

1/4 cup all-purpose flour

1/2 teaspoon ground cinnamon

1/4 teaspoon ground nutmeg

6 medium tart cooking apples, peeled, cored, sliced

Place 1 dough into ungreased 9-inch pie plate. Combine all filling ingredients *except* apples in bowl. Add apples; toss lightly to coat. Spoon apple mixture into prepared crust. Add remaining dough over filling. Trim, seal, and flute edge. Cut 5 or 6 large slits in crust. Brush with 1 tablespoon melted butter; sprinkle with 1 tablespoon sugar. Cover edge of crust with 2-inch strip aluminum foil. Bake in a hot oven 35 minutes; remove foil. Continue baking 10 to 20 minutes or until crust is lightly browned and juice begins to bubble through slits in crust. Cool pie 30 minutes; serve warm.

Seed sample books were not only lovely to look at but full of information on the apple's pedigree, growing statistics, and shelf life.

ANISIM

IOWA BEAUTY

PATTEN'S GREENING

Four of the Best
Hardy Apples.

(PAINTED FROM NATURE)

FLORENCE CRAB

SEEDS,
NURSERY
STOCK,
AND BULBS.

Farmer Seed and Nursery Co. Faribault, Minn.

STECKER CO. ROCHESTER N.Y.

"The Minnetonka,"
Minnesota's Great Seedling Apple

The "Minnetonka" Apple

AS HARDY AS AN OAK. IT THRIVES AND YIELDS
WHERE ALL OTHER VARIETIES FAIL. FRUIT VERY LARGE.
FLESH TENDER, CRISP, SUB ACID. THE IDEAL COOKING AND CHOICE DESSERT APPLE.
SEASON LATE, KEEPING TWO MONTHS LONGER THAN THE WELL KNOWN WEALTHY
PROPAGATED, OWNED AND CONTROLLED BY US.

WE GUARANTEE EVERY TREE OF THE MINNETONKA VARIETY PURCHASED FROM US UNTIL IT PRODUCES
A BUSHEL OF FRUIT AND WILL REPLACE FREE OF CHARGE ANY TREE THAT MAY DIE
BEFORE THIS RESULT IS OBTAINED. WHAT STRONGER RECOMMENDATION CAN WE GIVE?

PRICES.

4 to 5 ft. trees - 75¢ each - 3 for $2.00 - 6 for $3.00 - 12 for $6.00
Mail Size, One Year Old - 40¢ each - 3 for $1.00 - 6 for $1.75 - 12 for $3.00
For History, Testimonials and Full Description of this
Famous Variety, See Other Side.

L.L. MAY & CO.
St. Paul, Minn

Apples, with their spherical shapes, pretty rose blush, and glossy green leaves, are satisfying to paint. Their inherent appeal tempted growers as they considered which little brown seedlings to buy.

Hot Coffee and Hot Chocolate

Lots of good, strong coffee was almost a requirement to survive in Minnesota's chilly climate. Artists created alluring images on sturdy containers that cooks wanted to keep. These catchalls stayed around kitchens to hold spoons or in workshops to hold supplies.

Images of animals or domestic scenes were common, but the fascination with American Indians was deeply typical of this and later eras. These images may have helped consumers forget the conquest that made Minnesota an agricultural powerhouse. Buyers remembered the intriguing graphics and would look for them again on grocer's shelves.

COFFEE AND COCOA FROSTING

3 cups confectioners' sugar
3 tablespoons unsweetened cocoa powder
2/3 cup butter, softened
3 tablespoons strong brewed coffee

Stir together sugar and cocoa powder.
In a medium bowl, beat the butter
until creamy; gradually beat in the sugar
mixture. Stir in the coffee and beat until
smooth and fluffy. Makes enough for
12 to 15 cupcakes.

CHAPTER 2
1900–1920

The new century brought an easier manner of living as well as new styles of art and design. Lavish Victorian decorations gave way to Arts and Crafts simplicity and Art Nouveau elegance. Fashionable clothing became more comfortable as the bustle and corset disappeared. The Nineteenth Amendment gave women the right to vote; the Wright brothers took off and the Titanic sank; Charlie Chaplin made his first movie, *A Dog's Life.* Change was in the air.

Artists drew inspiration from organic shapes and simple forms, and design took on an effortless appearance. Wrappings for spice tins, canned foods, and other packaging became a source of uniquely regional art, displaying connections to both local landmarks and faraway places. Area seed growers printed evocative paintings on their catalogs and seed packets that were circulated nationwide.

Cooks modernized their lives with up-to-date kitchen designs, and cumbersome old methods rapidly fell away. Recipes provided detailed instructions for making unusual vegetable and molded salad combinations or classic ribbon tea sandwiches and also offered hints on how to use newly imported aromatic spices.

As World War I brought the economy to a standstill, saving food became everyone's patriotic duty, and health was uppermost in people's minds. Still, Minnesota companies grew throughout the period and emerged as major suppliers of many of the nation's important food products. As life eventually returned to normal, newly developed foods and unusual canned and packaged goods led to irresistible aromas wafting from the kitchen stove.

Keeping Food Cold

In the days before electricity came to residences, big blocks of ice were the only way to keep food cold. Homemakers worked constantly to keep ahead of spoilage.

Painters used cool scenes of well-watered gardens by lakeside settings to portray a sense of crispness and freshness. A late-Victorian arbor and ornate ironwork added elegant surroundings for the hardworking iceman.

PEANUT ICEBOX COOKIES

1 cup packed brown sugar	2 3/4 cups flour
1 cup butter, softened	1/2 teaspoon baking soda
1 egg	1/2 teaspoon salt
1 1/2 teaspoons vanilla	3/4 cup peanuts, chopped

Beat together brown sugar, butter, egg, and vanilla in large bowl. Stir in flour, baking soda, and salt. Mix in peanuts. Divide dough in half and shape each into a roll two inches in diameter. Wrap and store in icebox until firm. Cut rolls into eighth-inch slices. Place on cookie sheet. Bake at 375°F for 6 to 8 minutes.

Made in St. Paul by White Enamel Refrigerator Company, Bohn Syphon refrigerators boasted handsome woodwork and easy-to-clean enamel linings. The nationally known company also delivered its cabinets to hotels, clubs, restaurants, yachts, and railroad cars.

Recipes

Old Home
Creamed
Cottage Cheese

Old Home Creameries
MINNEAPOLIS - ST. PAUL

Keeping time with architectural fashion, cottage-style houses began appearing in ads and cookbooks at the turn of the century. With fluffy clouds and shaded woodlands surrounding a Craftsman cottage, a colorful cookbook cover expressed the freshness of the Old Home Company's creamery products.

HAWAIIAN SURPRISE

8 slices pineapple

1 pound Old Home cottage cheese

salt, pepper, paprika

lettuce

french dressing

mayonnaise

cherries

Drain pineapple slices and dry thoroughly. Combine Old Home cottage cheese with salt, pepper, and paprika to taste. Spread thick on each slice of pineapple. Then press 2 slices together with cheese between. Chill well, cut in wedge shapes, and pile on crisp lettuce. Pour over french dressing and serve with mayonnaise. Dot with cherries.

A Little Book for a Little Cook

P illsbury's 1905 cookbook for children was an Art and Crafts showpiece. The cover featured a three-dimensional modeled clay illustration, while pen and ink interior drawings led children on a tale through the pages to learn early cooking skills. The Arts and Crafts movement valued handcraftsmanship over machine-age mass production.

MUFFINS

1/3 cup butter

1/4 cup sugar

1 egg

1 cup milk

2 cups Pillsbury's Best flour

1/4 teaspoon salt

4 teaspoons baking powder

Beat butter, sugar, and egg until creamy. Add milk a little at a time, gradually stirring in flour sifted with salt and baking powder. Grease muffin pan, heat slightly, put in mixture, and bake in quick oven.

FUDGE

1 1/2 tablespoons butter

1 cup sugar

1/4 cup milk

2 tablespoons molasses

1 ounce chocolate

1/2 teaspoon vanilla

Melt butter in a granite pan. Add sugar, milk, and molasses, stirring gently until sugar is dissolved. Boil slowly without stirring for 5 minutes. Add chocolate square and stir until melted. Boil again until a little of the mixture dropped in cold water seems brittle. Remove from range, add vanilla, beat until mixture begins to thicken, then pour into a buttered pan. Cool and cut into squares.

> "This world is so full
> of a number of
> things,
> I am sure we should
> all be as happy
> as kings."

The fashionable Arts and Crafts–style dining room displayed handcrafted woodwork and decorative objects common to the era. The fetching pen and ink illustrations were similar to those in children's books by Beatrix Potter with her quaint stories and pretty watercolor pictures.

Cooking with Pillsbury's Best flour was the focus of the book, but youngsters dressed in their company best provided examples of period trends—inside the kitchen and out.

The Spice City

Who would expect a Minnesota town to be the capital of spices in the Midwest? Yet shipments of pungent seasonings came up the Mississippi River from all over the world for a variety of companies—all located in Winona. The aromatic spices were featured in painterly catalogs and packaged in eye-catching tins and boxes. Then the door-to-door salesmen went to work.

Dr. Ward's 1912 "almanac" was primarily a cookbook with ideas on how to use spices. In charming soft and subtle colors, illustrations of the four seasons guaranteed that the booklet would be kept around all year.

The catalog also offered liniments for people and horses, pills for colds and stomachaches, and cures for any number of common and unknown ailments. If all those failed, details on the phases of the moon might help.

Ward's spice tins featured beautiful motifs in Art Nouveau, an internationally popular and elegant style characterized by flowing curves, linear designs, and natural forms. The label was a perfect combination of Japanese-inspired organic shapes, stylized flowers, and sophisticated Tiffany-like swirls and leaves that surrounded the top of the can.

Ward's fostered the craving for worldly seasonings. Palm trees and Chinese spice boats were sure to attract the eyes of cooks wanting more exotic flavorings for their meals.

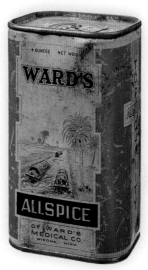

ALLSPICE CHUTNEY

2 large tart apples, peeled, cored, and chopped

1 small onion, chopped

1/4 cup vinegar

1/4 cup packed brown sugar

1 tablespoon grated orange peel

1 tablespoon grated fresh ginger

3/4 teaspoon allspice

Combine all ingredients in a medium saucepan. Bring to a boil, stirring well; reduce heat and simmer, covered, for 40 minutes. Uncover and continue to simmer until excess liquid has cooked off. Cool. Cover and refrigerate for up to 2 weeks.

McConnon and Company

If good cooking could guide families along "the rainbow road to health and happiness," McConnon and Company had the recipe. In addition to spices and flavoring extracts, the book also offered toilet articles, household necessities, veterinary goods, and products for physical ailments, in both humans and animals.

The classic rural midwestern bungalow and barn design brought a bold color palette to the McConnon book cover. In the 1900s, farmhouse cottage architecture became a sought-after style for a growing population of homeowners, both rural and urban.

The Rainbow Road to Health and Happiness

McCONNONS BOOK
WINONA, MINN.
MEMPHIS, TENN.

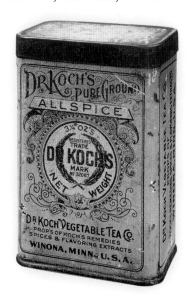

AUNT SUE'S GINGER SNAPS

One cup sugar, one cup butter or lard, one cup molasses, one teaspoon soda in one-half cup boiling water, two tablespoons McConnon's ginger, one tablespoon McConnon's cinnamon, one-half teaspoon McConnon's cloves. Mix thoroughly, drop in tins, and bake quickly.

PICKLES

One dozen large store cucumbers, one teaspoon McConnon's cinnamon, one teaspoon McConnon's cloves, three pounds sugar. Cut cucumbers in thick slices, put in layer of cucumbers, then layer of spice and sugar in jar alternately till jar is full. Keep warm but not hot on back of stove for twenty-four hours, then cool. They will be ready for use in two days.

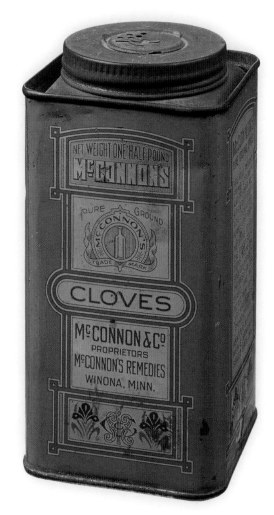

McConnon's spice labels were designed in the Arts and Crafts style of linear shapes with simple folk art illustrations. The flower and leaf image at the bottom of the label was similar to the famous William Morris designs created in beautiful screen prints for fabrics and wallpapers.

Dr. Koch Vegetable Tea Company in Winona commissioned spice labels that used a wide variety of typestyles. Combinations of different typographic elements were becoming fashionable, and American typesetters would make font and typestyle an important element of design for the new century.

J. R. Watkins

At home in Plainview, Minnesota, in 1868, J. R. Watkins made a one-of-a-kind pain reliever to soothe the aches of hardworking men and women. He sold his popular concoction door to door and soon hired salesmen to expand the business. In 1885, baking materials found their way into catalogs, and the Watkins Company, now in Winona, eventually employed a person-to-person sales force in the thousands.

The artistically rendered catalogs were kept handy in kitchens for ordering flavorings and spices and in parlors for browsing the latest recipes, almanac tables, health ideas, and household tips.

Impressionist painter Pierre-Auguste Renoir once asked, "why shouldn't art be pretty?" His paintings were light-hearted, filled with people, and brimming with life. The 1917 Watkins illustrator may have been influenced by Renoir's focus on painting figures, particularly women, in outdoor settings.

Teatime on a wicker-furnished porch as the Watkins man approached, a roadster tooling along a shaded Mississippi roadway—scenes on these Watkins covers answered Renoir's call for pretty art.

WAITING FOR THE WATKINS MAN

WATKINS

50th Anniversary
ALMANAC
HOME DOCTOR
AND COOK BOOK
1917

THE
J. R. WATKINS
MEDICAL CO.
WINONA, MINN.
U. S. A.
BRANCHES
NEW YORK, MEMPHIS,
HOUSTON, SAN FRANCISCO,
WINNIPEG.

FRENCH CHOCOLATE CREAMS

Two cups granulated sugar, one-half cup milk or water, boil hard five minutes; flavor with Watkins vanilla. Stir briskly until it creams sufficiently to mold into the size desired. Dissolve Baker's chocolate over steaming teakettle, then drop in one cream at a time until covered with chocolate. Lay on platter to dry.

Decorative pictures enticed customers from grocery-store shelves, and packages for G. F. Foster products were the most extravagant by far. The motto "spices that talk" practically guaranteed this product would perk up a meal. Artistically spectacular, Foster labels called out to shoppers, "Pick me!"

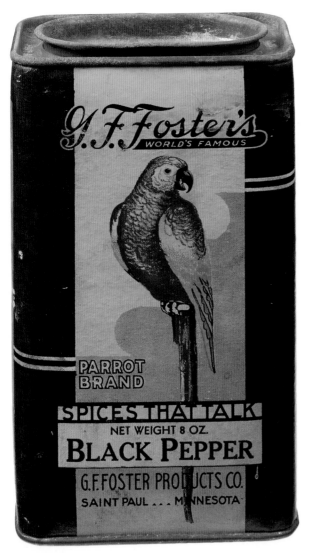

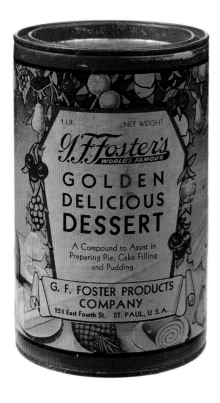

Golden Delicious Dessert was a baker's secret ingredient, easy to add to pie filling, cakes, cookies, puddings, and ice cream. Recipes on the package advised that just a couple of tablespoons would make a variety of delicious desserts. A border of brightly illustrated fruit hanging over a table of pies and cakes would have inspired cooks of any ability.

Before condiments were commercially available, cooks prepared their own concoctions at home. Catsup was the all-time favorite, but it took a long time to cook—sometimes up to four hours.

TOMATO CATSUP

One peck ripe sound tomatoes in quarters. Boil five minutes, cool, strain through coarse sieve. To this juice add: three medium-size onions chopped, one full cup granulated sugar, one-quarter cup salt, one-quarter pint white vinegar, one-half ounce catsup spice placed in a muslin or cheesecloth bag. Boil until desired thickness is obtained.

Spice users always wanted the freshest seasonings available, and importers trumpeted neighborhood connections in the competitive spice market. Architectural drawings of the St. Paul Winter Carnival's ice palace sat side by side with quaint, familiar homes. Local flowers put a little garden color on pantry shelves in winter as well as summer. Other miniature paintings looked beyond the region, featuring a travelogue of national and world landmarks.

Trillium BRAND
1½ Ounces Net Wt.
BLACK PEPPER
PACKED FOR
FRIEDRICH & KEMPE CO INC
RED WING, MINN.

THISTLE BRAND
STRICTLY PURE
CREAM TARTAR
SLOCUM-BERGREN CO.
MINNEAPOLIS, MINN.

McMURRAY'S
LAND O'LAKES BRAND
PURE GROUND
ALLSPICE
2 Ozs.   Net Wt.

FULLERTON'S
SPICES
SAGE
PACKED BY
F. L. FRARY & CO.
(EST. 1885)
MINNEAPOLIS, MINN.

McCORMICK, Behnke & Co.
PALACE BRAND
TRUE
CAYENNE
PEPPER
ABSOLUTELY PURE.
¼ lb. FULL WEIGHT.

TRUE SPICES

Home Brand
CINNAMON
MANUFACTURED BY
Griggs, Cooper & Co.
ST. PAUL, MINN.

OLD FAITHFUL BRAND
CLOVES
PACKED FOR
V. R. IRWIN & CO.
ST. PAUL, MINN.

HEALTHY TURMERIC GINGER TEA

2 cups water

1 teaspoon turmeric powder

1 teaspoon ginger powder

honey

lemon slices

Bring water to a boil in a small teapot. Add turmeric and ginger and simmer for 8 to 10 minutes. Pour tea into cup; add honey and lemon to taste. For centuries, this combination had been a cleansing, curing medicinal tea.

Farmer Seed Company

Founded in 1888 with a firm grasp on which growers to attract for grain sales, Farmer Seed Company of Faribault, Minnesota, featured golden fields of wheat on its catalog covers. As the wheat belt expanded, hundreds of Minnesota mills grew to keep pace, many claiming to be the largest in the world.

Farmer Seed covers imitated the painterly Barbizon school of art popularized by French artist Jean-François Millet. Millet pursued historical realism in his paintings of harvest scenes, peasant figures, and golden fields of rural landscapes. Those images seemed right at home in Faribault. Other covers celebrated the midwestern work ethic or ever-popular American nationalism.

WHEAT BERRY SALAD

1 1/2 cups hard wheat berries
1/2 cup chopped walnuts, toasted
1 cup chopped green apples
2 stalks celery, finely chopped
3/4 cup dried cranberries, chopped
2 scallions, white and green parts, chopped
2 tablespoons olive oil
2 tablespoons apple cider vinegar
2 tablespoons orange juice
salt and pepper

In a large pot, combine the wheat berries and enough salted water to cover by 2 inches. Bring to a boil and cook uncovered for 1 hour or until tender. Drain and cool. In a large bowl, combine the wheat berries, walnuts, apples, celery, cranberries, and scallions. Mix olive oil, vinegar, and orange juice; season to taste with salt and pepper; toss gently with salad.

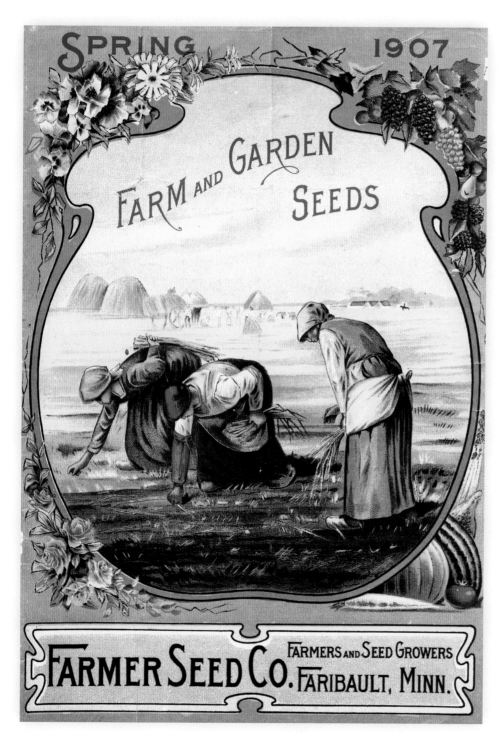

Peasant women were frequently the subject of Millet paintings. In *The Gleaners*, now on display at the Musée d'Orsay in Paris, three women collect bits of grain after the harvest. The 1887 image reflects the backbreaking labors of the French peasantry and infuses the women with a noble, monumental strength.

Crispy Rosettes and Crusty Breads

It took heavy-duty irons to make rosettes, and Alfred Andresen had the sturdiest and most beautifully designed by far. A heated iron dipped in batter, then plunged in hot oil, produced delicious, crispy rosettes. It was fussy work, but after a meal of French peas in a crunchy shell, diners might still ask for a rosette for dessert.

Rosettes from hot irons slipped straight to the painter's canvas, where they emerged as picture-perfect examples to inspire skillful cooks.

FRENCH-STYLE PEAS

1 1/2 tablespoons butter

6 lettuce leaves, finely shredded

1 small onion, thinly sliced

2 pounds fresh peas, shelled

2 teaspoons sugar

3/4 teaspoon salt

2 tablespoons water

Melt butter in a saucepan; add lettuce, onions, and peas; sprinkle with sugar, salt, and water. Cover tightly and cook over low heat 25 minutes or until peas are tender. Mix carefully and serve.

"Rosettes"
PATTY WITH FRENCH PEAS

KORNU KOPIA
KRUMB KAKES

"Rosettes"
STRAWBERRIES WITH CREAM
DECORATED

Echoing the whimsical style of Swedish artist Carl Larsson, this Gold Medal flour ad connected with Minnesota Scandinavians. Larsson's watercolor illustrations celebrated family, with children often gathered around tables laden with Swedish breads and sumptuous smorgasbord dishes. His inspirational room creations became the epitome of Swedish interior design. Larsson's artworks are celebrated around the world in museums, in art galleries, and on perpetually popular greeting cards.

Eventually

WASHBURN·CROSBY'S

GOLD MEDAL FLOUR

Why Not Now?

BE SURE YOUR BREAD IS MADE FROM GOLD MEDAL FLOUR

Gibson Girls and World War I

Charles Dana Gibson was one of America's most popular illustrators at the turn of the twentieth century. His fashionable Gibson Girls were forward looking, optimistic, witty, and urbane. This *Sunday Magazine* cover painted by Albert Steiner was a study in Gibson Girl style. Peeling an orange while dressed in a flowing gown, with upswept hair and an aristocratic attitude, this girl stood for what many American women aspired to be.

Gibson was a committed supporter of World War I. He and other famous illustrators like James Montgomery Flagg, Joseph Pennell, and N. C. Wyeth donated their time to create some of the most enduring posters of the war. From these well-designed images, poster art evolved into a category of its own.

ORANGE CAKE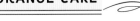

3 eggs, separated

2/3 cup sugar

1/4 teaspoon salt

1 teaspoon grated orange rind, plus more for topping

1 teaspoon orange juice

1/4 cup cold water

1/4 cup unbleached flour

1/2 teaspoon baking powder

powdered sugar

Place whole egg into cup; fill with egg yolks to 1/2 cup line. Add to sugar in mixing bowl; beat very light. Add salt, orange rind, juice, and water. Fold in flour and baking powder. Pour into pan and sprinkle with powdered sugar and grated orange rind. Bake in 300°F oven 45 minutes. Test. Invert until cold.

SUNDAY MAGAZINE
Of the MINNEAPOLIS JOURNAL
MINNEAPOLIS, MINN.
JANUARY 3, 1909

MAC AND CHEESE

1 (8–ounce) box elbow macaroni

1/4 cup butter

1/4 cup all-purpose flour

1/2 teaspoon salt

black pepper

2 cups whole milk

2 cups shredded cheddar cheese

1 cup toasted bread crumbs

Cook elbow macaroni in boiling salted water according to package directions. Drain. Melt butter in saucepan over medium heat; stir in flour, salt, and pepper until smooth, and cook about 5 minutes. Slowly pour milk into flour mixture, stirring until mixture is smooth and bubbling, about 5 minutes. Add cheese and stir until melted. Fold in macaroni until well coated. Serve with topping of toasted bread crumbs.

Similar to an eye-catching and informative wartime poster, the Young-Quinlan Company department store cookbook featured a Gibson Girl look-alike. She may be cooking a pot of macaroni and cheese, a popular win-the-war meal. Patriotism and sacrifice were watchwords as meatless recipes became the heart of many meals.

Flour and corn were valuable commodities during wartime, and Minnesota companies joined in the conservation effort with cooking tips to save on these and many other foods—all to benefit the troops stationed overseas.

CUSTARD CORN CAKE

2 eggs

1/4 cup sugar

1/2 cup flour

1 teaspoon baking soda

1 teaspoon salt

1 2/3 cups cornmeal

1 cup sour milk

1 cup sweet milk

2 tablespoons butter

1 cup cream

Beat the eggs and sugar together thoroughly. Sift the flour, baking soda, and salt together and mix with the cornmeal. Mix all the ingredients but the butter and cream. Melt the butter in a deep ovensafe pan, using plenty on the sides. Pour in the batter, add cream (without stirring), and bake 20 to 30 minutes. When cooked, there should be a layer of custard on top of the cake. For economy's sake, milk may be used in place of the cream.

JOHNNYCAKE

3 cups cornmeal

1 cup flour

2 teaspoons baking soda

1 teaspoon salt

3 cups buttermilk

2 tablespoons molasses

2 eggs, beaten

Mix and sift dry ingredients; add the buttermilk and molasses slowly; add the eggs and beat all together for 2 minutes with a broad spoon. Bake in 2 pans for 30 minutes in a moderate oven.

Standing back of
UNCLE SAM

CREAM OF WHEAT
is Economical – One
package will make ten
quarts of cooked food

E PLVRIBVS VNVM

War Time Recipes

MINNESOTA HISTORICAL SOCIETY
Pamphlet Collection
Presented with the compliments of
KOMO FLOUR

A confident baker using Komo flour graced the cover of the St. Paul Milling Company's recipe book. Her proudly held cake was probably made following cookbook advice on how to use substitutes for wheat during the war years.

As a direct communication between product and buyers, package design was an important part of commercial art. Typestyles featured attention-getting elements, and high-contrast colors helped buyers remember brands.

Butter cartons sported images of the cows and barns, fields and lakes typical of Minnesota dairy country, and children made for memorable images as well.

Milton Dairy, maker of Star Brand butter, thought butter worthy of sculpture. E. Frances Milton carved elaborate pieces of butter statuary, and in the early 1900s, figures of children, dogs, and everyday scenes appeared at the Minnesota State Fair in a custom octagon glass refrigerator case built by her husband, Thomas Milton.

BREAD PUDDING

8 slices white bread, torn into pieces

1/2 cup raisins, optional

2 cups milk

1/4 cup butter

1/2 cup sugar

2 eggs, slightly beaten

1 tablespoon vanilla

Heat oven to 350°F. Combine bread and raisins (if using) in bowl; set aside. Combine milk and butter in 1-quart saucepan. Cook over medium heat until butter is melted. Pour milk mixture over bread; let stand 10 minutes. Stir in sugar, eggs, and vanilla. Pour into greased 1 1/2–quart casserole. Bake 40 to 50 minutes or until set in center.

BUTTERY WHISKEY SAUCE

1/2 cup sugar

1/2 cup butter

1/2 cup heavy cream

1/4 cup whiskey or bourbon

Combine ingredients in small saucepan. Warm over low heat, stirring until sauce is gently boiling. Pour over bread pudding.

Season's Greetings from
MILTON DAIRY CO.
St. Paul, Minn.

Seed Packet Art

When seed packets arrived, thoughts of healthy salads with crispy greens inspired a quick tilling of the garden soil—including the planting of dandelion seeds. Dandelions were considered desirable salad greens as well as beautiful backyard flowers.

SAVORY DANDELION SALAD

1/2 pound torn, very young dandelion greens, before buds form

1 cup red onion, thinly sliced

2 tomatoes, chopped

1/2 teaspoon dried basil

salt and pepper to taste

In a medium bowl, toss together dandelion greens, onion, and tomatoes. Season with basil, salt, and pepper. Toss with warm bacon dressing or oil and vinegar mixed with a little sugar.

SUMMER SAVORY SALAD

3 tomatoes, cut into small wedges

1/4 cup fresh lemon juice

1 teaspoon sugar

2 teaspoons olive oil

2 teaspoons chopped fresh savory

1/4 teaspoon salt

1 garlic clove, minced

Place tomatoes in a medium bowl. Combine remaining ingredients, stirring with a whisk. Pour dressing over tomatoes; toss gently to coat. Let stand 1 hour, stirring occasionally.

MAY'S NORTHERN GROWN SEEDS

LETTUCE. TENNIS BALL, BLACK SEEDED.

LECHUGA. Pelota para juego de Raqueta Semilla Negra

STANDARD FOR PURITY

L.L. MAY & CO. St. PAUL, MINN.

5 CENTS

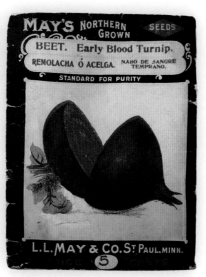

MAY'S NORTHERN GROWN SEEDS

BEET. Early Blood Turnip.

REMOLACHA Ó ACELGA. NABO DE SANGRE TEMPRANO.

STANDARD FOR PURITY

L.L. MAY & CO. St. PAUL, MINN.

5 CENTS

Seed packets tempted buyers with appealing art, usually healthy images of the vegetables themselves. Artistic license was given to illustrate foods in ideal proportions and at ready-to-pick ripeness.

L. L. May & Co. of St. Paul sowed its seeds far and wide, advertising vegetable names in English as well as Spanish for export.

PARSNIP
HOLLOW CROWN
SWEET, FINE GRAINED

15 CENTS

FARMER SEED & NURSERY CO.
FARIBAULT, SEEDS MINNESOTA.

RADISH
CAVALIER

550

SHORT TOP–HIGH QUALITY

15 CENTS

FARMER SEED & NURSERY CO.
FARIBAULT, SEEDS MINNESOTA.

RADISH
EARLY FRENCH BREAKFAST
GOOD SIZE—CRISP AND TENDER

15 CENTS

FARMER SEED & NURSERY CO.
FARIBAULT, SEEDS MINNESOTA.

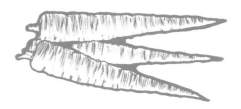

Peas, Please

Of all the vegetables in the garden, peas provided great artistic opportunities, and painters rose to the challenge. Gangly vines held plump peas in bright green pods to engage buyers looking for seeds and canned goods. Beans too offered painterly possibilities.

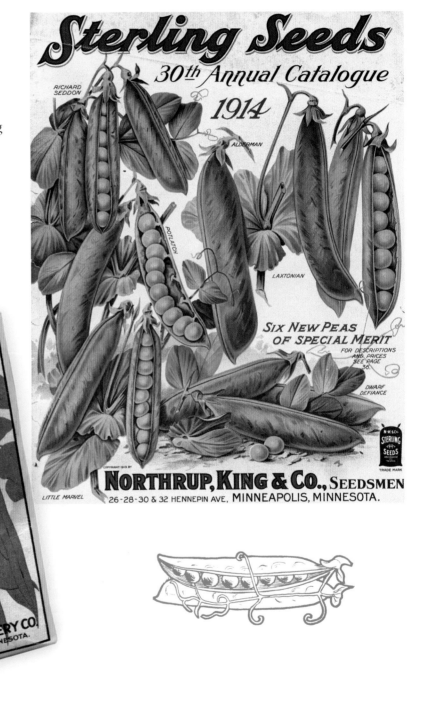

CREAMED PEAS

2 cups green peas

2/3 cup water

1/4 teaspoon salt

3 tablespoons butter

2 tablespoons all-purpose flour

1 tablespoon sugar

1/3 cup cream

In a medium saucepan, combine peas, water, and salt. Bring to a boil and cook until tender; stir in butter. Mix together flour, sugar, and cream. Add to peas. Cook over medium-high heat until thick and bubbly.

Forward-thinking advertising by Russell-Miller Milling Co. elevated its flour to "fine art" status. Occident flour was promoted as high quality but more expensive. The company put together many of Minnesota's most innovative illustrations and art-related marketing themes.

With remarkably creative ingenuity, Occident portraits in the style of the internationally acclaimed John Singer Sargent appeared in national magazines. Beautiful women in pearls and frothy dresses stood out from dark, moody backgrounds and radiated prosperity, a beautiful fit with Occident's declaration of "Costs More—Worth It."

TEATIME RIBBON SANDWICHES

HAM FILLING

1/2 cup finely chopped cooked ham

2 tablespoons mayonnaise

2 tablespoons sweet pickle relish

1/2 teaspoon prepared mustard

EGG FILLING

2 hard-cooked eggs, chopped

2 tablespoons mayonnaise

2 tablespoons finely chopped celery

salt and pepper

SANDWICHES

8 slices white bread

4 slices whole wheat bread

Combine ingredients for each filling in individual bowls; set aside. Trim crusts from bread, creating equal-sized slices. Place 4 white slices on a cutting board. Spread each with 1/4 ham filling. Top with 1 slice whole wheat bread. Spread with 1/4 egg filling. Top with 1 slice white bread. Wrap each sandwich in plastic food wrap; refrigerate at least 1 hour. Slice sandwiches into thirds. Garnish with cucumber slices, parsley sprigs, or celery leaves.

OCCIDENT
FLOUR

Costs More
—Worth It

Ads printed with carved, gilded frames furthered the notion that these paintings were indeed fine art.

Take-Me-Home Can Labels

Fresh produce arrived by truck at local companies that canned the fruit and vegetables for delivery to grocery shelves. To attract shoppers, illustrators and lithographers were hired to design tantalizing depictions of each can's contents. A thin coat of varnish on the label brightened up the colors, and the prettiest picture often won top place in the cart.

Neighborhood names and landmarks caught shoppers' eyes. The University brand label displayed University of Minnesota buildings along with an owl in a graduation cap. Who could resist supporting local education?

WHIPPED PRUNE SOUFFLÉ

5 egg whites

1/4 teaspoon cream of tartar

1/2 cup sugar

1/2 teaspoon lemon zest

3/4 teaspoon lemon juice

1 teaspoon vanilla

1 cup canned pitted prunes, pureed

Preheat oven to 325°F. Butter a 4-cup soufflé dish or 8 individual custard cups. Beat the egg whites with the cream of tartar to a stiff peak. Slowly add sugar, lemon zest, lemon juice, and vanilla. Fold the egg whites into the pureed prunes. Spoon the mixture into the prepared dish or cups. Bake for 20 to 25 minutes. Serve warm with topping of berries and mint leaves.

NET WEIGHT
1 LB. 4 OZ.

PILLSBURY HALL

ARMORY

CHEMICAL

ALL GOODS UNDER
THIS BRAND ARE OF
EXTRA STANDARD QUALITY

PACKED FOR **WINSTON-HARPER-FISHER CO.** MINNEAPOLIS, MINN.

Sadly, few of the vintage labels survived since most were tossed out with the garbage; those that live on were mostly overruns buried in storage until someone uncovered them, appreciated the unique art, and decided they were worth saving.

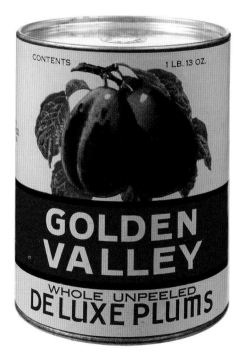

Can and Box Labels

Early grocery shelves offered a lineup of beautiful illustrations that resembled a miniature art show. Pen and ink drawings with watercolor washes highlighted flourishing fields and orchards, with farmers wheeling out fresh vegetables or packing ripe produce to complete the picture.

Stacked boxes at the grocery store displayed a portrait gallery of personalities. Cute kinfolk, like the farmer's daughter on Minnesota spaghetti and early Creamette boxes, called out to moms looking for dinner ideas.

CREAMETTE HEARTY ITALIAN MEAT SAUCE

1 1/2 pounds lean ground beef or bulk Italian sausage

3/4 cup chopped onion

2 cloves garlic, finely chopped

1 (28–ounce) can tomatoes

1 (8–ounce) can tomato sauce

1 (6–ounce) can tomato paste

1 tablespoon beef bouillon

2 teaspoons sugar

1 1/2 teaspoons Italian seasoning

In large skillet brown meat; pour off fat. Add onion and garlic; cook and stir until tender. Stir in remaining ingredients. Simmer uncovered 45 minutes, stirring occasionally. Serve over hot cooked spaghetti with grated cheese.

Seed Sack Art

Illustration styles for seed sacks were bold and graphic so printing clarity would hold up on rough fabrics. Here as elsewhere, businesses used Native American faces to sell products. Regional scenes from farms to lakes were common, and typography was a dominant design element.

CRUNCHY SKILLET CORNBREAD

1 1/4 cups coarsely ground cornmeal

3/4 cup all-purpose flour

1/4 cup granulated sugar

1 1/2 teaspoons salt

2 teaspoons baking powder

1/2 teaspoon baking soda

1 3/4 cups buttermilk

2 eggs, lightly beaten

8 tablespoons butter, melted

Preheat the oven to 425°F and place a 9-inch cast-iron skillet in to heat while you make the batter. In a large bowl, mix together cornmeal, flour, sugar, salt, baking powder, and baking soda. Whisk in the buttermilk, eggs, and most of the melted butter, reserving about 1 tablespoon for the skillet. Carefully remove the hot skillet from the oven. Reduce oven temperature to 375°F. Swirl bottom and sides of the hot skillet with the remaining butter. Pour batter into skillet and place in the center of the oven. Bake until the center is firm, about 20 to 25 minutes.

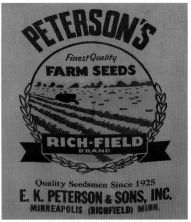

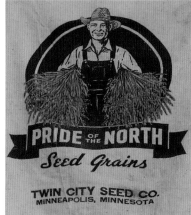

Soda Labels

If cool graphics could conjure up thirst, Minnesota soft drink companies offered relief in ale, cider, and soda. Intriguing type and jazzy graphics appealed to everyone from hip teens to reminiscing oldsters. The bright and cheerful labels were a potpourri of "printer's art" from books of designs that could be copied by publishers.

HOT APPLE CIDER

12 cups apple juice

1 tablespoon ground cinnamon

1 tablespoon honey

1 teaspoon vanilla

12 whole cloves stuck in a whole orange

Pour apple juice into a large pot. Stir in cinnamon, honey, vanilla, and orange. Warm over low heat for 30 minutes or more. Serve hot or cold. Sneak in a little bourbon for extra warmth.

CREAM SODA

2 cups sugar

juice of 1 lemon

1 1/2 vanilla beans, split, seeds scraped and reserved

soda or seltzer water

Place sugar and 1/4 cup tap water in a medium saucepan. Heat over medium-high heat until sugar is caramelized. Slowly add 2 cups water, lemon juice, and vanilla bean and seeds, and bring to a boil. Remove from heat and let stand for 2 hours. Discard vanilla bean and pour syrup in airtight bottles. To serve, fill a tall glass with ice cubes and add 1 1/2 ounces of syrup; top with sparkling water and stir gently to combine.

CONTENTS 24 FL. OZ.

LUX

LIME SODA

ARTIFICIALLY COLORED AND FLAVORED
MADE WITH BEST CANE SUGAR
AND PUREST INGREDIENTS OBTAINABLE

JOHN W. LUX CO.
WHOLESALE GROCERY SPECIALTIES
ST. PAUL, MINNESOTA.

DREWRY & SONS. BEST QUALITY
TRADE MARK
SARSAPARILLA
CONTENTS 9½ FL.OZ.
WILL KEEP IN ANY CLIMATE ST.PAUL, MINN.U.S.A.

SWEET APPLE CIDER

Contents 7 Fl. Oz.

DREWRY & SONS,
ST. PAUL, MINN.

PURITY STRENGTH
OUR DRINKS HAVE BEEN THE STANDARD
PREPARED WITH PURE SPRING WATER BY
RED CROSS
BOTTLED BY THE LATEST SYSTEM BECOMES
FOR FORTY YEARS
CAP. ABOUT 12 OZ.
GUARANTEED
BY
DREWERY & SONS
UNDER THE FOOD
AND DRUGS ACT
JUNE 30,
1906.
SERIAL NO. 6405

Cream Soda

DREWRY & SONS

ST. PAUL, MINN.

CLEANLINESS EXPERIENCE

CHAPTER 3
1920–1940

The modern era in the United States began in 1920. For the first time in history more Americans lived in cities than in rural areas, and the average house was being updated dramatically.

The lights came on. Kitchens were wired with electricity, telephones connected neighbors near and far, sinks had running water, and refrigerators stored cold foods safely. Better roads and affordable automobiles opened opportunities to travel, broadening Americans' horizons.

The Jazz Age, the Roaring Twenties, and styles of Art Deco and Streamline Moderne influenced all areas of life. Flapper-style cooks wore avant-garde fashions while creating state-of-the-art food preparations. F. Scott Fitzgerald wrote *The Great Gatsby,* the hit movie was *Gone With the Wind,* and lifestyles in America were full of enthusiasm and creativity.

Some of the most beautiful cookbook art and ingenious advertising programs were developed during this time. Cooks scrutinized trendy publications that featured the latest recipes, kitchen products, and cooking equipment. Cooking was fun, and abundant and colorful recipe books included helpful hints for entertaining. Homemakers found time to make fancy molds, crisp salads, and creamy desserts that brought compliments from guests.

But for all its glamour, the era was not without its challenges. Prohibition changed dining for more than a decade, making a glass of wine or a fancy drink a treat of the past for most Americans. Then the stock market crashed, and the country entered the Great Depression. The Works Progress Administration provided jobs and incomes to the unemployed and trailblazing programs for artists, musicians, and writers.

Eventually, the nation began to emerge from economic despair. Surely, good times were just around the corner.

Fun in the Kitchen

At the start of the 1920s, cookbook designs engaged readers from the front cover to the very last pages, and food artists found new visual opportunities to illustrate finished recipes.

Cookbooks became plentiful and included entertainment ideas along with intriguing recipes for party fare. The country was in an optimistic mood, and people wanted to have fun with their cooking. Meals would become more adventurous than in the past.

Tried Recipes Made With Excelsior Butter-Krust Toast

SHRIMP WIGGLE

1 tablespoon chopped onion

1 teaspoon butter

1/2 cup tomatoes

1 cup Butter-Krust Toast crumbs

2 cans shrimp

1 cup milk

salt and pepper

Cook onion in butter; add tomatoes and the Butter-Krust Toast crumbs. Add shrimp, cut up, then milk; season with salt and pepper; pour in pudding dish and bake 30 minutes.

EXCELSIOR
BAKING
COMPANY
MINNEAPOLIS, MINNESOTA

Up-to-the-minute grocers stocked new varieties of ingredients previously not available at the corner store as cutting-edge recipes suggested new flavors to try for everyday meals.

At a rapid pace, American houses were equipped with electricity for refrigerators, gas for stoves, and sinks with running water. Pursuing the culinary arts became easier and more interesting.

With an early Art Deco–style kitchen on the cover, a Ceresota pamphlet offered hints on keeping those new kitchens pristine. Cookbook art turned to graphic design for inspiration, with simple lines, bold shapes, and shadowed fonts. The pamphlet also included avant-garde recipes.

SELF-FROSTING LEMON PIE

1 pie crust

1 cup sugar

2 tablespoons unbleached flour

1/4 cup melted butter

3 egg yolks, well beaten

1 lemon

1 cup milk

3 egg whites, beaten stiff

Line pie plate with crust, brush with cream, and bake at 450°F for 15 minutes. Mix sugar and flour; stir in butter and egg yolks. Add juice of lemon and its grated rind. Pour in milk. Fold in egg whites. Pour into baked shell. Reduce oven temperature to 325°F. Bake about 45 minutes, until set. Cool.

COOKERY KINKS

♦ MEN LOVE PIE ♦

As Prohibition arrived in the 1920s, a glass of wine or a fancy drink was hard to find, but diners on the Big Stone Canning cover didn't seem to mind. They wore classic Deco fashions—she in a cloche hat and, probably, with seams in her silk stockings. And even in Ortonville, Minnesota, thousands of miles from Paris, the couple would have enjoyed a French corn casserole.

Rows of perfect kernels in a lineup of neat cobs became a decorative design element on the canning booklet cover. Hot or cold, corn was always a welcome addition to a meal.

DEVILED CORN EN CASSEROLE

Make a cream sauce of two tablespoonfuls of butter, three tablespoonfuls of flour, and one cupful of milk; cook until it thickens, stirring constantly; season with salt, paprika, a little dry mustard, a few grains of cayenne, and one tablespoonful of sugar. When the sauce is made, add one can of Douthitt's kernel corn and two well-beaten eggs, also one tablespoonful of Worcestershire sauce. Pour all into a buttered casserole and cover with crushed bread crumbs. Dot top with butter. Bake until a light brown. Chopped parsley or one minced green pepper adds color to this dish, and a meringue of egg white is ornamental.

Easy Cooking

Standing next to a modern stove or a sink with running water, Pillsbury's flapper-era cooks were happily on the forefront of enormous change. In *Great Gatsby* style, hemlines rose and chemise dresses brought new comfort for day and evening wear. The Roaring Twenties were about modernism and experimenting with new fashion and design; the art and culture of the past were about to be altered dramatically.

The Pillsbury Company was milling flour on the Mississippi River overlooking St. Anthony Falls. A total of seven mills, including the A Mill that became the world's largest flour mill, housed state-of-the-art machinery that increased the company's output. Pillsbury's cookbooks and advertising were among the most creative in the industry, and the baking contests attracted national attention.

In the Art Deco style of bold whirlpool circles, vibrant color, and oversized lettering, Pillsbury's cookbooks and packaging were on the cutting edge of modern design for the coming years.

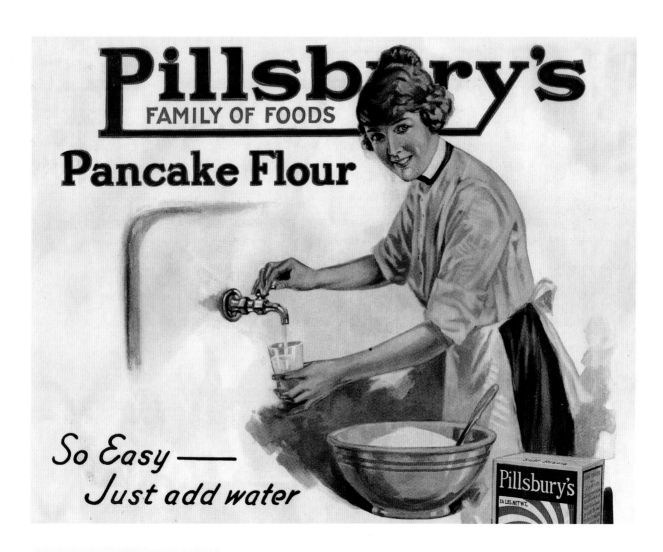

CHICKEN EN CASSEROLE

1 1/2–pound whole chicken	1 tablespoon flour
1/2 cup butter	1 tablespoon chopped parsley
1 stalk celery, chopped	1 teaspoon salt
1 can mushrooms	1/2 teaspoon pepper
1 carrot, chopped	2 cups boiling water
1 onion, chopped	

Steam the chicken until tender. Melt butter in a frying pan, add all the vegetables, cook 5 minutes, and then add the flour. Add seasonings to hot water, pour into frying pan, and cook 5 minutes. Put the chicken in a casserole, dredge with flour, dust with salt and pepper, and pour the contents of the frying pan over it. Bake at 400°F for 25 to 30 minutes, until chicken is thoroughly browned.

Fine Art Food Paintings

For centuries, still life paintings of food have been a favorite subject of artists and art buyers. Old world–style paintings of baked goods made with Airy Fairy flour are reminiscent of the works of the great Dutch and Flemish masters who catered to popular fine art tastes of the sixteenth century. As the artists explored familiar elements of peasant life and favorite foods, their richly pigmented artworks brought them recognition and fame. Airy Fairy artists included period table settings to enhance their beautiful food illustrations.

COOKIE CUTTER COOKIES

1/4 cup shortening

1/2 cup sugar

1 egg

1/2 teaspoon vanilla

2 tablespoons milk

1 1/4 cups Airy Fairy flour

1/2 teaspoon baking powder

pinch salt

Cream the shortening; add sugar gradually. Add well-beaten egg and vanilla. Add milk alternately with flour, baking powder, and salt. Chill the dough for an hour or longer. Roll very thin and cut with cookie cutters. Bake at 350°F for 5 to 10 minutes.

The Fine Art of Cakes

Airy Fairy oil painters excelled at the effects of light and texture on fluffy fillings and nubby frostings. Cakes shown in lush brushstrokes nestled against dark, romantic backgrounds would inspire readers to look for their mixing bowls.

AIRY FAIRY BUTTER CAKE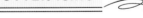

1/3 cup butter

1 cup sugar

2 eggs

1 teaspoon vanilla

1/2 cup milk

1 1/2 cups Airy Fairy flour

2 teaspoons baking powder

1/4 teaspoon salt

Cream the butter until very soft. Add sugar gradually, beating it in well so that the mixture will be light and creamy. Add well-beaten eggs and flavoring. Add milk alternately with flour, baking powder, and salt which have been sifted together. Beat the batter until the ingredients are thoroughly blended, about 2 minutes. Turn into 2 (8-inch) layer cake pans and bake at 375°F for 25 to 30 minutes.

BUTTER ICING

2 tablespoons butter

1 1/2 cups confectioners' sugar

3 tablespoons hot milk or cream

1/2 teaspoon vanilla

Soften the butter and mix in the sugar. Add enough liquid to make of the right consistency to spread. Add flavoring and beat until smooth.

Cake Baking Made Easy

With **Airy Fairy**

Delicious Cakes for Every Occasion from **6** Foundation Recipes

Price 25 cents

Birthday cakes rendered in the masters' style brought smiles to the faces of children of all ages. The frosting invites the swipe of a finger; the cookies tempt small hands to snatch. Just a taste, please.

Pillsbury in the Twenties

In the 1920s, plein air, or open-air, painting was immensely popular. Artists brought their easels and painting supplies to outdoor locations and painted the world before them. Close attention was paid to the play of natural light and shadow and the changing reflection of colors. This appealing art style made its way into food company promotions of the era, too. In one enticing Pillsbury advertisement, the energy of a family picnic communicates plein air outdoor flavor in a picturesque painting. The perspective leads the eye back to a grandmother transferring Pillsbury breads from a Model T. Newly affordable automobiles changed picnics forever.

CHICKEN SALAD SANDWICHES

2 cups cooked chicken, diced into half-inch cubes

1 tablespoon lemon juice

1 1/2 cups white celery, diced

1 teaspoon salt

1/2 teaspoon white pepper

mayonnaise

whipped cream

capers

lettuce

Sprinkle chicken with lemon juice and place on ice. When ready to serve, mix the chicken with celery; dust with salt and pepper. Mix the mayonnaise with whipped cream to taste, and mix into the salad. Sprinkle with capers. Serve on lettuce between pieces of fresh bread.

BASIC YELLOW CAKE

2 1/2 cups all-purpose flour

3 teaspoons baking powder

1/4 teaspoon salt

1 1/4 cups sugar

3/4 cup butter or margarine, softened

1 teaspoon vanilla

3 eggs

1 cup milk

Heat oven to 350°F. Grease 2 (8- or 9-inch) round cake pans with shortening; lightly flour. In medium bowl, mix flour, baking powder, and salt. In large bowl, beat sugar and butter with electric mixer on medium speed until light and fluffy, scraping bowl occasionally. Beat in vanilla and eggs until well blended. Alternately add flour mixture and milk, beating well and scraping bowl after each addition. Pour batter evenly into pans. Bake 27 to 35 minutes, until toothpick inserted in center comes out clean. Cool in pans 10 minutes. Remove from pans; place on wire racks. Cool completely, about 1 hour. Fill and frost as desired.

CHOCOLATE ICING

1/2 cup butter, cubed

4 ounces unsweetened chocolate, chopped

3 3/4 cups confectioners' sugar

1/2 cup whole milk

1 1/2 teaspoons vanilla

In a small saucepan, melt butter and chocolate over low heat. Cool slightly. In a large bowl, beat confectioners' sugar, milk, and vanilla until smooth. Gradually add melted chocolate mixture, beating until light and fluffy. Spread between layers and over top and sides of cake.

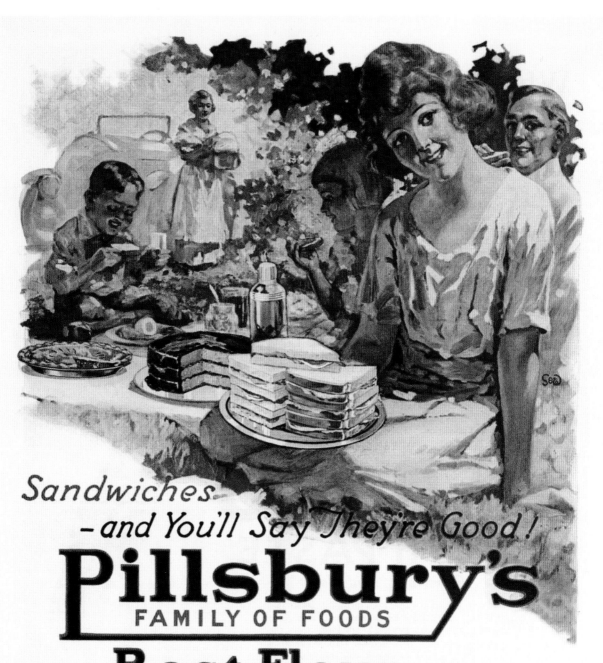

Sandwiches
— and You'll Say They're Good!

Pillsbury's
FAMILY OF FOODS
Best Flour

Log Cabin Syrup

Minnesota grocer Patrick Towle lived in the small village of Forest Lake. When he introduced his Log Cabin syrup in 1887, he named it in honor of his childhood hero, President Abraham Lincoln, who grew up in a log cabin.

Many Log Cabin recipes included illustrations of warm-from-the-oven dishes that tempted cooks to try the syrup in unusual ways, like Minnesota apple pork chops with fried cornmeal mush and a generous pour of maple syrup.

FRIED CORNMEAL MUSH

1 cup cornmeal

4 cups boiling water

1 teaspoon salt

1 egg, beaten

bread crumbs

Log Cabin syrup

Cook cornmeal in boiling salted water for 30 minutes. Pour into greased bread pan or baking powder tin. Cool, slice, dip in egg and crumbs, and fry in hot fat. Serve with Towle's Log Cabin syrup.

LOG CABIN GRAPEFRUIT

Towle's says: "Try grapefruit sweetened with Log Cabin syrup instead of sugar. If you've never tried this you'll be pleasantly surprised. The maple flavor blends deliciously with the fruit juice."

Toasty-colored paintings warmed the hearts of magazine and journal readers in the 1930s. This artist provided a wintry glimpse into an active woodland scene with velvety colors, soft tones, and bright sun on the roof of a sugar bush shack. Babies, pets, and horses drew readers into the genial activities of turning maple tree sap into barrels of sweet syrup.

CABIN FUDGE

1 cup Log Cabin syrup

2 cups sugar

2 tablespoons butter

1/2 cup milk

Boil all ingredients together until a soft ball forms when dropped in cold water. Remove from the fire and cool; then beat until creamy. Add nuts if desired. Roll to a half-inch thick and cut in squares.

Recipes Olde and New

Holidays were all about food, and local markets were just around the corner to provide meats and recipes that would build family traditions. Ovens sent forth savory aromas, heralding holiday gatherings that would become lasting memories of good times.

Inspired by such warm recollections, the artist for Walter's Meat Market fashioned nostalgic winter festivities in falling snow complete with glowing window lights. Winter scenes have been painted by countless artists throughout the centuries.

BAKED PORK CHOPS

Cook two cups whole small white onions in butter until the onions are soft, but not brown. Take one tablespoon chopped parsley, yolks of two eggs, well beaten, juice of one lemon, salt, and pepper. Mix all these ingredients together. Place the onions carefully in the bottom of a shallow baking dish; pour the above mixture over them. Lay over the top pork chops that have been seasoned. Spread with buttered crumbs and bake for about one hour or until the chops are well cooked.

Holiday Greetings

FROM

WALTER'S MEAT MARKET
742 Grand Ave., St. Paul, Minn.

The city of Minneapolis granted the newly formed Minneapolis Gas Light Company a franchise in 1870 to provide gas service to the area. In a remarkable feat of endurance, this Home Service Department recipe book survived decades of Minnesota's cold winters, testament to collectors' determination to keep traditional holiday recipes intact.

CHRISTMAS DIVINITY

2 cups sugar
1/2 cup white syrup
1 cup water
2 egg whites, beaten
1/2 cup walnuts, chopped
1/4 cup red maraschino cherries, cut
1/4 cup green maraschino cherries, cut
1/2 teaspoon vanilla

Combine sugar, syrup, and water and boil to soft ball stage. Pour slowly over egg whites, beating constantly. Continue beating until mixture begins to lose its gloss. Immediately add walnuts, cherries, and vanilla. Drop individual pieces off teaspoon onto waxed paper.

Sweets for Sweeties

Expressive drawings of lovely ladies decorated boxes of chocolates that appealed to the fairer sex as well as to admirers looking for a kiss. With names like Sweetest Maid, local candymakers tempted any customer's sweet tooth.

CHOCOLATE-COVERED CHERRIES

60 maraschino cherries with stems

3 tablespoons butter, softened

3 tablespoons corn syrup

2 cups confectioners' sugar

1 pound melting chocolate for candy making

Drain cherries and set aside on paper towels to dry. In a medium bowl, combine butter and corn syrup; stir in confectioners' sugar and mix into a dough. Wrap each cherry, stem up, in about 1 teaspoon of dough. Chill until firm. Melt chocolate in a heavy saucepan over low heat. Dip each cherry in by its stem, and place on waxed paper–lined baking sheets. Chill until set. Store in an airtight container.

NACACO
CHOCOLATES

National Candy Company
ST. PAUL FACTORY

NACACO
CHOCO

National Candy Company
ST. PAUL FACTORY

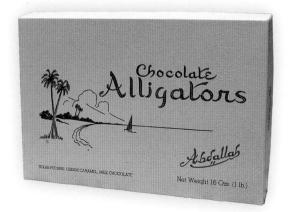

Chocolate Alligators

Abdallah

TEXAS PECANS, CREAM CARAMEL, MILK CHOCOLATE

Net Weight 16 Ozs. (1 lb.)

The busy Minneapolis corner of Lake and Hennepin was sweetly sugarcoated when Albert Abdallah began making candy there in 1909. In big copper kettles set over an open flame, he stirred together the finest ingredients he could find. The Minnesota company has flourished ever since through the gifted hands of four generations—and its cooks still use the same copper pots.

Founded in 1909 by five brothers, Pearson's at first distributed candy made by other confectioners. Soon, the Minneapolis company wanted to be in business for itself, and in 1912 it debuted the Nut Goodie, followed in 1933 by the Salted Nut Roll, Mint Patties, and many others. Visitors stocked up on these midwestern treats, carrying them to the coasts to the grateful joy of transplants who remembered them longingly.

Pearson's
SALTED NUT ROLL NET WT. 2 1/4 OZ.

Pearson's
CHOCOLATE COVERED
MINT PATTIE
PEARSON CANDY CO. • ST. PAUL, MINNESOTA
5¢

HAS STOOD THE TEST OF TIME

Pearson's NUT GOODIES 5¢
from the HOUSE of PEARSON

Fashionable Food

Sweets, in all their delightful forms, became the most sought-after treats in the Deco era. Yet, a slender, boyish look was easy for women to maintain with dropped waists and silky fabrics. And in a bonus to the fashion conscious, dresses came ready made and ready-to-wear from the department store.

As a hostess satisfied her guest's sweet tooth by serving chunky cakes with plump frostings, a painter for Pillsbury put a spotlight on both the fashions and the cakes, the artistic sleight of hand conjuring thoughts of high style along with sugary temptations.

CLASSIC RED VELVET CAKE

CAKE

1 1/2 cups granulated sugar

2 large eggs

1 1/2 cups vegetable oil

1 (1–ounce) bottle red food coloring

2 teaspoons vanilla

1 teaspoon white vinegar

2 1/2 cups Pillsbury all-purpose flour

2 tablespoons cocoa powder

1 teaspoon baking soda

1/2 teaspoon salt

1 cup buttermilk

FROSTING

1 (8–ounce) package cream cheese, softened

1/2 cup butter, softened

1 teaspoon vanilla

3 1/2 cups powdered sugar

Preheat oven to 350°F. Coat 3 (9-inch) round cake pans with nonstick cooking spray. Beat granulated sugar and eggs together in a large bowl with electric mixer on medium speed until combined. Add oil, food coloring, 2 teaspoons vanilla, and vinegar. Beat until smooth. Add flour, cocoa, baking soda, salt, and buttermilk. Beat 2 minutes, scraping bowl occasionally. Pour into prepared pans. Bake 25 to 30 minutes or until toothpick inserted in center comes out clean. Cool 5 minutes. Remove from pans. Cool completely.

Beat cream cheese and butter in large bowl with electric mixer on medium speed until creamy. Add 1 teaspoon vanilla and powdered sugar. Beat until light and fluffy, about 2 minutes. Frost cake as desired.

Buzza Company

George Buzza opened his printing company in Minneapolis in 1907. A commercial artist by trade, he became a pioneer in the innovative use of color and exotic, unusual papers. Five floors in his Lake Street building were soon filled with artists, designers, printers, engravers, and gold leafers who designed thousands of books and greeting cards. Pretty pictures sold, sentimental verses were popular, and demand was high for Buzza's books, cards, and other publications.

MAPLE RUSSE

1 cup maple syrup

1/2 cup light cream

4 egg yolks

1 teaspoon powdered gelatin

1 cup heavy cream, whipped

strips of sponge cake

Combine maple syrup and light cream and scald over hot water. Beat egg yolks light, pour into the hot maple mixture, return to heat, and cook 5 minutes longer, stirring constantly. Add gelatin softened in cold water; cool. Then beat till very creamy. Fold in heavy cream. Serve in frappé glasses lined with sponge cake strips. Sprinkle tops with chopped toasted almonds and coconut, if desired.

RHUBARB ESCALLOP

1 quart chopped, unpeeled rhubarb

2 cups sugar

3 cups soft bread crumbs

1/4 cup melted butter

Butter a baking dish, and put in a layer of rhubarb mixed with sugar. Spread on this a layer of the crumbs mixed with melted butter. Continue until all is used, making the last layer crumbs. Cover and bake 45 minutes at 350°F to 375°F. Then uncover to brown.

SOUR CREAM DROP CAKES

3/4 cup butter

1 1/2 cups packed brown sugar

2 eggs

1 cup sour cream

1/2 teaspoon mace

1 teaspoon baking soda dissolved in 1 teaspoon boiling water

2 teaspoons baking powder

2 1/2 cups flour

1/4 teaspoon salt

nuts

Cream butter and sugar, beat in eggs and cream, and sift the dry ingredients into the first mixture. Drop by small teaspoonfuls on buttered pans, keeping 2 inches apart; press a nut meat into each, and bake 15 minutes at 350°F to 375°F.

The Roaring Twenties were on a roll, and Buzza recipe book covers featured sophisticated designs to quickly draw the attention of would-be chefs. Fanciful illustration by Carrie Dudley explored the unexpected theme of a suave flamenco player and his partner dressed in billowy fabrics. The picture conjured the desired image of delectable Dainty Desserts, and the books sold fast. Printed with metallic gold ink, the recipe booklet could hang from its tasseled cord on a kitchen wall as a piece of art.

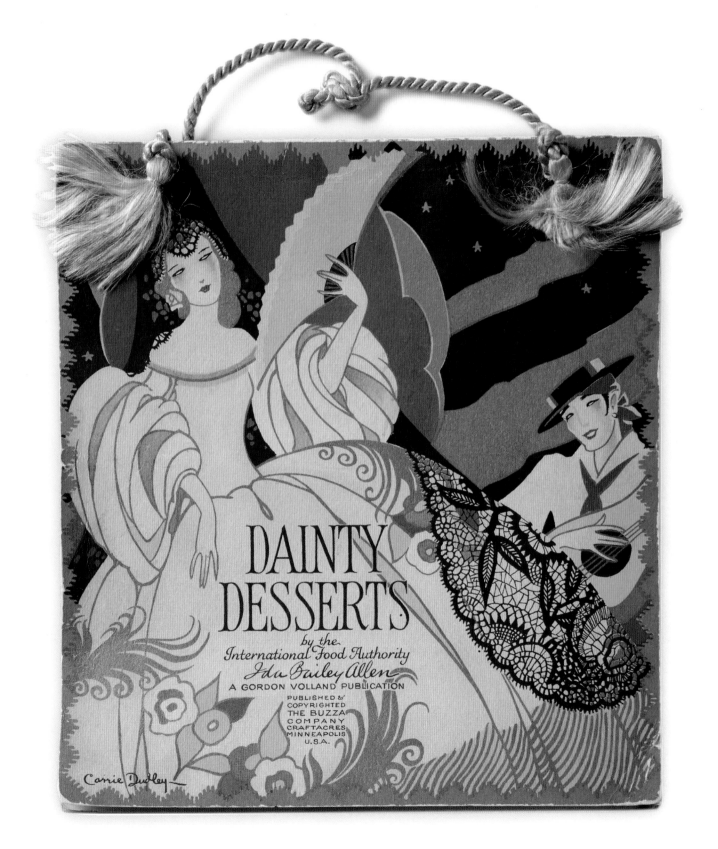

DAINTY
DESSERTS
by the
International Food Authority
Ida Bailey Allen
A GORDON VOLLAND PUBLICATION

PUBLISHED &
COPYRIGHTED
THE BUZZA
COMPANY
CRAFTACRES
MINNEAPOLIS
U.S.A.

Carrie Dudley

Buzza for Lunch and Tea

Eating well appealed to stylish folks of all sorts. A Buzza Company cookbook for luscious lunches and tasty teas featured an elegant period illustration that complemented the recipes inside. Edwardian finery of powdered wig, hoop skirt, and lacy gloves was no doubt designed to attract a gourmet's interest in the "International Food Authority's" exotic recipes. With a background of metallic gold, the fanciful illustration was created with easy flowing line work and flat fields of color.

Ida Bailey Allen, a nationally famous food editor and radio personality during the 1920s and '30s, developed recipes for Buzza cookbooks.

STUFFED LOBSTER

3 cups diced, cooked lobster meat

3 tablespoons butter

3 tablespoons flour

1 teaspoon salt

1/2 tablespoon minced parsley

3/4 teaspoon Worcestershire sauce

1/2 tablespoon lemon juice

1/3 cup bread crumbs, plus more for topping

1 1/2 cups light cream

2 hard-cooked eggs, chopped fine

watercress

Wash and dry six little lobster shells. Melt butter, add flour, seasonings, crumbs, and cream, and stir till boiling; add the eggs and lobster and heap in lobster shells. Spread with additional fine bread crumbs moistened with butter, and bake till browned at 375°F, about 15 minutes. Garnish with watercress.

BAKED SHRIMP-STUFFED TOMATOES

6 medium tomatoes

3 tablespoons butter

2 cups broken cooked shrimps

2 diced pimientoes

2 diced sweet green peppers

1 teaspoon Worcestershire sauce

2 tablespoons chili sauce

1 tablespoon lemon juice

bread crumbs

Remove the stem ends from the tomatoes and cut in halves crosswise. Scoop out and reserve the pulp, and dust the tomatoes with salt and pepper. Melt the butter, add all the remaining ingredients and the tomato pulp, and cook about 5 minutes; heap the halved tomatoes with this mixture, place in buttered muffin pans, sprinkle with coarse bread crumbs, moisten with melted butter, and bake 25 minutes at 350°F to 375°F. Serve in nests of rice or on toast.

PEACH CUPCAKES

2 tablespoons butter

1 1/4 cups sugar

2 eggs, beaten

1/3 teaspoon salt

1 cup chopped ripe peaches

2 1/2 cups flour

4 teaspoons baking powder

1 cup milk

Cream the butter; add the sugar, eggs, and salt. Stir the peaches into the flour and the baking powder. Add to the first mixture alternately with the milk. Transfer to oiled cupcake pans, and bake at 375°F about 20 minutes.

LUSCIOUS
LUNCHEONS
AND
TASTY TEAS
by the
International Food Authority
Ida Bailey Allen
A GORDON VOLLAND PUBLICATION
PUBLISHED AND
COPYRIGHTED BY
THE BUZZA COMPANY
CRAFTACRES
MINNEAPOLIS, U.S.A.

Carrie Dudley

Party Cakes

For home bakers, making party cakes could take up a whole afternoon, but the artistic gratification was worth it—maybe! The cake itself had to be delicious, and the decorations needed to be of the ooh-and-aah variety.

Illustrators might be challenged by velvety icing and embroidery-like adornments, but such embellishments would bring admiration for a cake maker—especially one looking to make a lasting impression.

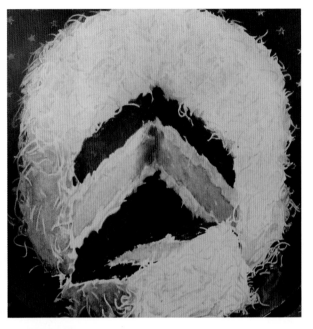

The Birthday Cake made this Gold Medal Way was a great success. It was so delicious husband asked for another piece and said he had the most wonderful little wife ever. The perfect cake made it a perfect day.

MARASCHINO CHERRY CAKE

1/2 cup shortening

1 1/4 cups sugar

1/2 cup broken nut meats

16 maraschino cherries, cut in quarters

2 1/4 cups plus 2 tablespoons Gold Medal cake flour

3 teaspoons baking powder

1/4 teaspoon salt

juice from 5–ounce bottle of cherries plus milk
to make 3/4 cup

4 egg whites

Cream shortening; add sugar gradually and cream together thoroughly. Mix nuts and cherries, and dredge with 2 tablespoons flour. Sift remainder of flour with baking powder and salt. Add to creamed mixture alternately with the liquid. Blend in the floured nuts and cherries. Fold in egg whites which have been beaten stiff but not dry. Pour into well-greased and floured 8-inch-square cake pan, and bake at 350°F for 50 minutes. Cool and frost with white icing and decorate with cherries, using strips of citron for leaves and stems to make cherry clusters.

Streamline Moderne Cooking

Streamline Moderne, or Art Moderne style, influenced all forms of design in the late 1920s. Human and animal forms were modernized, buildings emphasized curving forms and long horizontal lines, and graphics followed with strong and sleek shapes. The Art Deco Chrysler Building and the Empire State Building were on the drawing board. Cooking methods followed the trend-setting modern style, as pressure cookers simplified cooking, table settings became streamlined, and recipes became less complicated.

SEND FOR THIS NEW EASY-TO-USE RECIPE BOOK WITH REAL ALUMINUM COVER

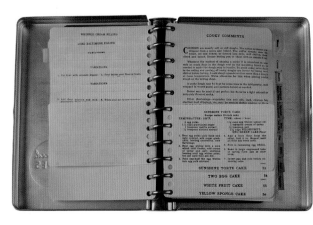

Enclosed in an aluminum box with a Streamline Moderne title treatment, this unusual Pillsbury cookbook opened as a ring binder holding hundreds of little pages. Modern recipes like molded and layered salads expanded a cook's horizon with trendy food combinations and sophisticated meal ideas.

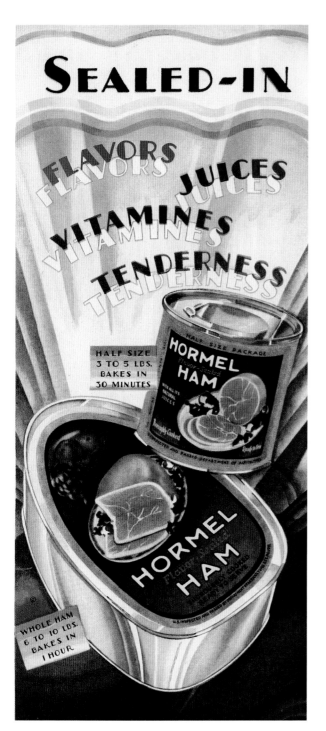

Designers paid attention to Streamline Moderne urbanity with the aerodynamic concept of motion and speed. Sleekly designed household products such as kitchen appliances and vacuum cleaners looked as though they could fly. This Hormel Foods ad followed those trends with sunburst patterns that drew the viewer's eyes straight to the gloriusly colored hams.

BAKED HAM WITH CURRIED FRUIT

1 slice ham, cut 1 inch thick
1/2 cup packed light brown sugar
1 cup fine, dry bread crumbs
3 tablespoons water
seasonings
2 teaspoons prepared mustard

Cut fat from ham; chop fat and mix with remaining ingredients. Wipe ham with damp cloth and place in baking pan. Cover ham with crumb mixture. Bake in moderate oven. Baste with juice in the pan at least 3 times during baking. Serve with curried fruit.

CURRIED FRUIT

Use halves of canned peaches, pears, or apricots and small slices of canned pineapple. Drain well from juice. Use as many pieces as will fill a deep casserole or baking dish. Pour over the fruit 1/2 cup melted butter mixed with 1 cup packed light brown sugar and 1 tablespoon curry powder; mix well. Bake 40 minutes in same oven with ham. Serve from dish in which it is baked.

Gedney Pickles opted for an Art Deco design—in both the label and the jar—that brought old-fashioned brines into modern times.

Meat for the Year

The Great Depression began after the stock market crash of 1929. Over the next years, rising levels of unemployment caused hardships throughout the country.

As consumer buying dropped, the Minnesota food industry survived with clever cooking incentives and artful advertising that brought a little cheer into homes during hard times. Light-hearted pen and ink drawings refreshed with watercolor washes, along with frugal meat-saving recipes, would keep the Housewife's Meat Calendar on the kitchen counter for the rest of the year.

BEEF HASH

Chop finely a small onion or two shallots. Melt one tablespoon butter in a small pan over a low fire. Add the onion and cook for five minutes. Remove fat and gristle from leftover beef. Dice beef and add two cups to the butter in the pan; add also two cups cold boiled diced potatoes. Season with one teaspoon salt, pepper, and powdered sweet thyme. Mix all together. Melt three tablespoons butter or clarified drippings in a frying pan. When hot, spread the hash mixture evenly in the pan. Cook until brown underneath, then turn. When brown on that side, fold, shaping as an omelet. Invert on a hot platter and garnish with parsley.

HOUSEWIFE'S MEAT CALENDAR 1929

JANUARY

FEBRUARY

MARCH

APRIL

MAY

JUNE

HOLIDAY GREETINGS
FROM
RYBAK'S
QUALITY MEATS
476 So. Snelling Ave.—Em. 2352
943 W. Seventh St.—Dale 1620

SWISS STEAK WITH VEGETABLES

salt and pepper

flour

1 thick piece round steak

2 tablespoons lard

1/2 onion, sliced

1 cup cooked tomatoes

1 cup diced carrots

1 cup finely cut celery

1 cup water

Add salt and pepper to flour and rub thoroughly into the meat. Brown meat in hot lard in frying pan. Add vegetables and water. Cover and simmer slowly for 2 hours.

BAKED LIMA BEANS AND BEEF

2 cups dried lima beans

1 pound beef chuck

2 tablespoons lard

3 sliced onions

2 tablespoons flour

1 1/2 teaspoons salt

pepper

dash mace

2 cups stewed tomatoes

Soak lima beans overnight. Then boil until soft in salt water and drain. Cut beef in small pieces and put in frying pan with lard and sliced onions. Stir in flour, salt, pepper, and mace. Place alternately in layers with the beans in a baking dish or casserole, spreading tomatoes between the layers. Barely cover with boiling water and cook for 3 hours in a moderate oven (375°F). Replenish the water as necessary to keep moist.

The WPA Years

In 1935, the Works Progress Administration began providing jobs and income to unemployed Americans. Almost every community in the United States had a new park, bridge, or roadside stop constructed by the agency.

The WPA program also employed artists, musicians, and writers for creative projects nationwide. Designers fashioned thought-provoking flyers on how to preserve and save on food; painters devised stunning murals to honor hard work. Minnesota artists created posters on recreational camping to promote the many revitalized state parks that were home to WPA-built hand-hewed stone structures, rustic log cottages, and piney campgrounds.

CAMPFIRE STEW

1 tablespoon vegetable oil

2 carrots, sliced

2 stalks celery, sliced

1 small onion, diced

2 cloves garlic, chopped

3/4 pound smoked sausage, sliced

2 (15–ounce) cans white beans, rinsed and drained

1 (14 1/2–ounce) can diced tomatoes, drained

1 teaspoon thyme

salt and pepper

Heat oil in a large skillet over fire. Add carrots, celery, onion, and garlic; cook until the onion is transparent. Add sausage and cook until brown. Add beans, tomatoes, thyme, salt, and pepper. Cover, and move to a low fire. Simmer, stirring occasionally, until vegetables are tender.

SHORE LUNCH

2 eggs

3/4 cup flour

1/2 cup cornmeal

1 teaspoon salt

1 teaspoon paprika

3 pounds walleye or other fish fillets

oil

Whisk eggs in bowl. In a large plastic bag, mix flour, cornmeal, salt, and paprika. Dip fish in eggs, then shake in flour mixture. Add oil to large cast-iron skillet placed over medium-hot fire. Fry fillets in batches 3 to 4 minutes on each side until fish flakes easily.

The hobby of arts and crafts moved into kitchens as putting together albums of "scraps" became a popular pastime that broadened artistic opportunities for collectors. Cooks gathered memories of treasured family dinners—favorite recipes, notes on successful menus, news clippings, and family photos—to make up their own personal cookbooks in memorable scrapbook style. Crescent Creamery stamps might adorn the pages with modern poster designs of the Jazz Age.

PEACH MACAROON PUDDING

peaches

1/4 pound crumbled coconut macaroons

1 egg

1 1/2 cups milk

1 tablespoon cornstarch

sugar to sweeten

1/2 pint cream

Slice fresh peaches into a deep dish to the depth of about 3 inches. On top of peaches put layer of macaroons. Make custard of egg, milk, cornstarch, and sugar. Cook in double boiler; when cool, pour over macaroons and peaches. Put in refrigerator to chill. Top with whipped cream.

HORMEL Ham and SPAM Luncheon Meat

Hormel Foods products have been on Minnesota dinner tables since 1891. That year, in an old creamery building on the Cedar River in Austin, Minnesota, George Hormel opened his first meat-packing operation. As business increased, other Hormel brothers signed on with the company and additional products joined the lineup. SPAM products made cooking fast and easy. With other convenience foods like canned stews, the company grew to national prominence.

HAM CRANBERRY GLAZE

1 (16–ounce) can whole cranberry sauce
1 cup packed brown sugar
1/4 cup orange juice
1/2 teaspoon ground cloves
1/4 teaspoon cinnamon
1/4 teaspoon allspice

Mix all ingredients over low heat until smooth. Serve with hot ham slices.

One artist envisioned a favorite family supper in a cheery dining room.

SPAM luncheon meat was introduced in 1937 and soon gained popularity around the world because of its extensive use by troops during World War II.

Artists had fun scripting cartoon conversations in 1930s advertising illustrations. Simply drawn and quickly understood, line drawings promoted the popularity of mealtime opportunities using SPAM luncheon meat.

GREAT AUNT VIVIAN'S REALLY GOOD HOT SPAM SANDWICH

4 thick slices white bread

1 can SPAM Classic, cut into 8 slices

8 slices American cheese

1 large tomato, sliced in 4 pieces

3/4 cup mayonnaise

paprika

Preheat oven to 350°F. Toast bread in toaster. Place on cookie sheet. Add to each slice of bread 2 slices of SPAM, 2 slices cheese, 1 slice tomato, and mayonnaise. Sprinkle with paprika. Bake for 30 minutes. Serve hot.

In the Land O'Lakes

In the early 1920s, the Minnesota Cooperative Creameries Association was formed with ideas about improving butter that was then made from sour cream and sold in tubs. The new butter, made from fresh, sweet cream and individually wrapped in one-pound boxes, soon became the national standard for packaging and quality.

In 1924, a name for the new butter—Land O' Lakes—was chosen in a local contest. The descriptive name became so popular that the cooperative itself later adopted it, becoming Land O'Lakes Creameries. It remains one of the largest producers of butter and cheese in the United States.

NEVER-FAIL CHEESE SOUFFLÉ

2 tablespoons Land O'Lakes butter

3 tablespoons flour

1/2 cup Land O'Lakes evaporated milk, undiluted

1/2 cup Land O'Lakes American cheese

salt and pepper to taste

3 Land O'Lakes eggs, separated

Melt butter; add flour and mix thoroughly. Add milk gradually, then cheese and seasoning. Remove from fire and add egg yolks, well beaten. Cool mixture and fold in stiffly beaten egg whites. Bake at 350°F for 25 minutes.

This 1935 recipe book cover shows only a hint of the famous aquatic visuals conjured up by the Land O'Lakes name. But the serene illustration of pine forests and rich farm-land bordering on clear blue waters could only reflect Minnesota's land of lakes. The dairyland fields are painted in beautiful autumnal colors on a background of real birch bark with a collage of twigs, pine branches, and leaves. The setting is suggestive of popular Hudson River School landscapes and those painters' ideals of romantic and scenic vistas.

Interior illustrations were drawn with a pointillism effect, with small dots blending together to create an image.

Land O'Lakes

The famous Land O'Lakes Native American woman holding the butter box was first painted in 1928 by illustrator Arthur C. Hanson for St. Paul's Brown and Bigelow. His concept has been redesigned and modernized many times over the years.

The original illustration is an example of the Droste effect, in which images can be repeated indefinitely. The woman holds a box of butter, with a picture of herself holding a box of butter, with a picture of herself holding a box of butter—and so on. This painting trick has been popular with artists for centuries.

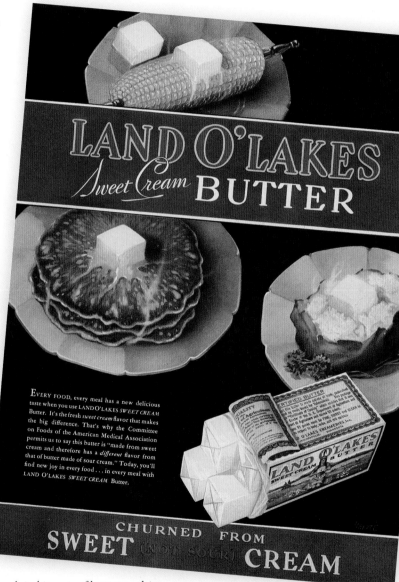

LAND O'LAKES
Sweet Cream BUTTER

EVERY FOOD, every meal has a new delicious taste when you use LAND O'LAKES *SWEET CREAM* Butter. It's the fresh *sweet cream* flavor that makes the big difference. That's why the Committee on Foods of the American Medical Association permits us to say this butter is "made from sweet cream and therefore has a *different* flavor from that of butter made of sour cream." Today, you'll find new joy in every food...in every meal with LAND O'LAKES *SWEET CREAM* Butter.

CHURNED FROM
SWEET (NOT SOUR) CREAM

Awash in big pats of butter melting on steaming corn, hot baked potatoes, and griddled pancakes, the enticing art tempted readers' appetites.

Fashion in the 1930s was full of glamour and style. Wardrobes were considered more feminine than the previous flapper-era styles of short skirts and boyish looks. Ad painters studied the attractive new fashions of jaunty hats and sleek, form-fitting fabrics to keep up on trends for readers of popular magazines.

A simple advertisement for butter became a fashion endorsement as glamorously attired guests gathered at a bread and butter board. Surely, more interesting luncheon offerings were cooking in the kitchen.

BUTTERSCOTCH COOKIES

1 cup Land O'Lakes butter	3 cups sifted all-purpose flour
2 cups packed brown sugar	1 teaspoon salt
2 eggs	1 teaspoon baking powder
1 cup finely chopped nut meats	1/2 teaspoon baking soda
1 teaspoon vanilla	

Cream together thoroughly the butter and sugar. Add the eggs, nuts, and vanilla. Sift together flour, salt, baking powder, and baking soda. Combine the moist and dry ingredients. Turn the cookie dough out on a floured baking board and divide it into several portions. Shape each portion into a long roll about 2 inches in diameter. Put in refrigerator until thoroughly chilled. When ready to bake, slice thin and bake at 350°F about 15 to 20 minutes.

In the early 1930s, Betty Crocker published favorite Bisquick recipes from famous movie stars, and their photos lit up smiles in the kitchen. Pictures of the glamorous screen idols and their hit films added a little movieland buzz to the task of cooking.

The splendid illustrations had a mouth-watering appeal that a browsing pastry chef would find hard to resist. Swirly creams and buttery biscuits jumped right off the page—and cooks could brag that the recipe was a favorite of a fabled movie star.

Easy-to-use Bisquick arrived in stores in 1931 and was an instant hit with on-the-go bakers.

Mary Pickford had an affection for strawberry shortcake; Claudette Colbert fancied peach shortcake.

FRUIT SHORTCAKE

2 tablespoons sugar
2 cups Bisquick
3/4 cup cream
crushed strawberries or sliced peaches

Add sugar to Bisquick. Stir in cream and mix well. Turn dough onto lightly floured board and knead gently to smooth up. Roll out three-quarter-inch thick. Cut with 3-inch cutter and bake in a hot oven, 450°F, for 12 minutes. Place fruit between layers and on top. Serve with whipped cream.

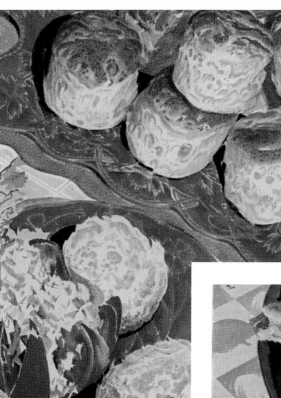

Gloria Swanson favored cheese Bisquicks, Clark Gable loved Bisquick griddle cakes with maple syrup, and Bette Davis enjoyed hunt club sandwiches.

HUNT CLUB SANDWICHES

Make Bisquick dough and roll out very thin, as for pie crust. Dot surface with four tablespoons butter. Fold so as to make three layers. Turn halfway around. Roll out half of the pastry to eighth-inch thickness to cover bottom of oblong pan, about 9x12 inches, and place in pan. Spread thickly with chicken and ham filling (see below). Cover with remaining dough rolled thin. Cut through in desired shapes, such as squares, diamonds, etc., but leave in place. Bake fifteen minutes in a hot oven, 450°F.

FILLING: To one and one-half cups cooked chicken cut up and flaked and three-quarters cup cooked ham cut in half-inch pieces, add four tablespoons top milk, three beaten egg yolks, and two hard-cooked eggs, chopped fine. Season with salt and pepper. Spread on pastry as directed.

Formal Sophistication

Interest in food was reaching new heights with designs of simplified elegance and formal style. Cookbook illustrations reflected a growing sophistication in art that was restrained and cultured. Americans began traveling more, dining out, and finding new tastes to try in their kitchens back home.

The 1937 world's fairs in New York and San Francisco brought food ideas from around the globe that were soon baking in ovens or cooling in refrigerators throughout the nation.

BAKED HAM WITH PEACH JUICE

Score the outside of a whole cooked ham into small squares; sprinkle with ground mustard and a little pepper. Stick a clove into each square; rub whole surface with a generous amount of brown sugar. Place in roasting pan, add two tablespoons bacon fat, one cup water, and about two cups peach juice, ginger ale, or cider; baste often while baking in uncovered roasting pan until hot.

FAMOUS TOMATO ASPIC SALAD

6 1/2 ounces lemon gelatin
1 cup boiling water
4 cups pure tomato juice
2 teaspoons salt
1/2 teaspoon white pepper
2 tablespoons vinegar
juice of 1 lemon
3 tablespoons minced onion
3/4 cup celery, cut fine
1/4 cup celery tops, cut fine

Dissolve gelatin in boiling water; add tomato juice. Add remaining ingredients and pour into 10 individual molds. Very delicious served with mayonnaise.

PERFECTION SALAD

3 1/2 ounces lemon gelatin
1 cup boiling water
1 cup cold water
juice of 1 lemon
juice of 1 lime
1/2 cup vinegar
4 cups shredded cabbage
2 pimientos, cut fine
1 cup diced celery
1/4 cup minced onion
salt and pepper to taste
stuffed olives, sliced

Dissolve gelatin in boiling water; add the other ingredients except olives. Place olives in bottom of mold. Pour one-quarter inch of mixture in mold. Set for 15 minutes. Then add the rest of the mixture, placing pimiento on top. Serve with russian dressing or mayonnaise, if desired.

MARY HUNT'S
SALAD BOWL

Minneapolis caterer Mary Hunt wrote a book in the 1930s to promote the importance of salads. An unusual list of ingredients encouraged cooks to get creative.

Pineapples, bananas, & cherries

Apples, celery, & walnuts

Oysters, grapefruit, & Tabasco

Oranges & Bermuda onions

Asparagus, pimiento, & peppers

Beets, cabbage, & horseradish

Shrimp, avocado, & tomatoes

Lobster, celery, & onion

Peas, cheese, & pickles

Apples, grapes, & nuts

Chicken, celery, & olives

Graphic design took a new direction when the flat poster art style became popular for cookbooks and cooking products.

Using bold shapes and strong colors, these pieces were designed to be both eye catching and informative. Flat colors, in the manner of silk-screened posters, called out for attention.

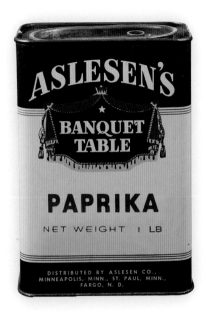

PAPRIKA OF VEAL

1 large onion, cut fine
2 tablespoons lard
2 pounds breast or shank of veal, cut in 1-inch cubes
salt and pepper
1 tablespoon paprika
1/2 cup sour cream
1 tablespoon flour

Brown onion in hot lard until it becomes slightly yellowed. Add veal cubes, and let brown. Sprinkle with salt and pepper; add paprika and enough hot water to cover. Cook slowly for 1 hour, then add sour cream and thicken the liquid with flour mixed with cold water. Serve in a rice ring.

HUNGARIAN LAMB STEW

2 tablespoons lard
2 small onions, chopped fine
2 pounds lamb shoulder, diced
salt and pepper
paprika
2 cups tomato puree
1 cup thick sour cream

Heat the lard. Add onion and diced meat which has been rubbed with salt and pepper and paprika. Brown the meat and then add the tomato puree. Let cook slowly for 2 hours, adding water when necessary. Just before serving add the sour cream and blend it well with the sauce.

Typography was an important part of poster art,
which featured clean lines and dense colors.

The Farmer's Wife

The popular *Farmer's Wife* magazine, first published in Winona, Minnesota, in the late 1800s, was eventually delivered to more than a million readers nationwide.

Tasty new recipes using locally grown crops were more than welcome in rural outposts, and a short story here and there brought new interest to a farmwife's day.

Skilled brushwork by storytelling artists yielded scenes that every homemaker could identify with—or dream about. Unusual perspectives and compelling colors were a welcome addition to the farmhouse coffee table.

GLAZED CARROTS AND ONIONS

1 dozen small young carrots	1/2 cup honey
1/2 pound small white onions	1 tablespoon hot water
1/4 cup butter, melted	

Precook carrots and onions in salted water approximately 10 minutes. Drain. Place in casserole. Combine remaining ingredients. Pour over vegetables. Bake in preheated 350°F oven for 20 minutes.

CRANBERRY-GLAZED YAMS

6 medium cooked yams or 1 large can whole yams

1 cup whole cranberry sauce

1/2 cup water

1/4 cup packed brown sugar

1/2 teaspoon grated orange rind

1 tablespoon butter

Peel cooked yams and cut in halves, or drain canned yams. Arrange in a buttered baking dish. Mix next 4 ingredients in saucepan and bring to a boil, cooking gently 5 minutes. Add butter and pour mixture over yams. Bake in preheated 350°F oven for 30 minutes, basting frequently with syrup in dish.

The Farmer's Wife
The National Magazine for the Country Woman

Another Ma Dunnaway Story • March 19

GARDEN NUMBER

The Farmer's **Wife**
The Magazine for the Country Woman

Dr. Paul Bartsch — Adventures of A Great Scientist • *October 1938* • New "Cal" Story — Lillard McGee Spins Another Yarn

Humer for Breakfast

Rhyming stanzas and energetic characters were a winning combination for breakfast seekers. With simple line work and subtle washes of delicate color, engaging drawings brought readers into stories that encouraged morning meals of flavorful hot cereal.

The Malt-O-Meal baby cartoon was similar to popular Kewpie dolls drawn by artist Rose O'Neill. The straightforward comic illustrations and sentimental poems drew viewers into the entertaining story.

MAGIC MUFFINS

1 1/4 cups all-purpose flour
3/4 cup uncooked Original Flavored Malt-O-Meal hot wheat cereal
1/2 cup sugar
3/4 cup milk
1/4 cup vegetable oil
1 egg
1 tablespoon baking powder
1/2 teaspoon salt
1 teaspoon vanilla (optional)

Preheat oven to 400°F. In a large bowl, combine all ingredients; stir together until ingredients are just moistened. Spoon into a greased or paper-lined 12-cup muffin pan, filling cups three-quarters full. Bake for 18 to 20 minutes or until toothpick inserted in center comes out clean.

C artoon art was a clever way to attract attention. Readers would spend time looking at the stories, appreciating the wit and humor and taking note of the product placement that brought a smile.

THE OCCIDENT PANTRY PALS INVITE YOU TO TRY
OCCIDENT FLOUR *Tested Recipes*

So simple
even a husband can do it!

"Gosh," says I to the little woman, "we never have hot biscuits!" To which says she, "As if I didn't have enough to do. Besides, I can't make a decent biscuit"...Well, you know me. Once I get an idea, I hang on. Saw some Bisquick at the grocer's. Sneaked a package home, and . . . Say, it's a cinch! Just dump some milk into the Bisquick and away you go. Simple. And the biscuits are swell!

* * *

Of all good words of tongue or pen The sweetest are these— "It's WHEATCAKES again!"

BREAKFAST NUT BREAD

2 cups sifted flour
3 teaspoons baking powder
3/4 teaspoon salt
1/2 cup sugar
1 cup walnuts, chopped fine
1 egg
1 cup milk

Sift flour, baking powder, salt, and sugar together. Add nut meats. Beat egg, mix with milk, and add to dry ingredients, mixing lightly. Pour into oiled bread pan. Let stand 20 minutes. Bake at 350°F for 45 minutes.

You'll need no clock to help awake the family when there's COFFEE CAKE!

Pancake Stories

I n the spirit of fun and amusement, the expressively illustrated story cartoons for Pillsbury pancake flour lured browsers to pause a minute and read about enchanting family dilemmas. Make-believe situations made viewers laugh at readily identifiable events of domestic life.

Cartoon artist George W. French created the "Ernest McGroucher" series for Pillsbury's pancake flour advertising. His drawings were designed to radiate the cheerful optimism of average people in everyday situations.

The emotionally charged facial expressions and animated poses provided an irresistible lure to look more deeply into the picture, and the clever message was one of memorable humor and unforgettable product recognition.

Ernest McGroucher, whose culinary efforts usually result in dismal failure, produces his Sunday morning masterpiece—Pillsbury's pancakes

Even mere man can turn out the perfect breakfast with Pillsbury's Pancake Flour. It's easy—simply add water or milk, and bake!

Pillsbury's PANCAKE FLOUR

Pillsbury's Pancake Flour

CHAPTER 4
1940–1960

The United States' entry into World War II threw the country into turmoil. As rationing went into effect, victory gardens sprouted up everywhere. Cooks put together clever food combinations for healthy menus. With shortages of paper and ink, cookbook and food advertising was a challenge as artists looked for ways to reach cooks and bakers with meal-saving recipes.

After the war, as life in the United States returned to normal, soldiers came home with money in their pockets and sweethearts on their arms. The economy began to boom as millions of people bought newly built homes in the suburbs and the population grew by leaps and bounds. Suburban sprawl attracted drive-ins, fast-food restaurants, TV dinners, and a great demand for easier food preparation.

Dazzling new designs energized cookbooks with enthusiastic illustrations and fanciful drawings that inspired interest in new food products. Trend-setting recipes came to modern kitchens that turned out dishes with exotic ingredients and seasonings from far-flung markets. The outlook was bright for experimentation in cooking.

With the introduction of pop art, abstract sensibilities were decidedly in. Designers embraced a new style of typography with dynamic typefaces, casual flowing script, and experimental graphic designs. Animated adventures gained traction with amusing and imaginative Disney cartoons, and cookbook cartoonists followed suit. Lively midcentury modern design became the new American art style.

The Space Age arrived in a hurry with jet aircraft, space rockets, and successful earth orbits. America immersed itself in the optimism of all the wonders the future would hold. In every aspect of popular culture, the new age altered past ideals and customs. Innovation in both food and art unfolded at an ever-more-rapid pace.

Green Giant in the Farm Fields

New products and informal ways of dining provided exciting alternatives in the 1940s. Expanding family farms bought bigger and better tractors, and increasing numbers of quality roads moved agricultural products to market swiftly and safely. Electricity, telephones, radios, and indoor plumbing revolutionized farm and city life. Americans were optimistic as the country climbed out of the Depression.

Advertising for companies like Green Giant was a study in fine art. Those in charge had the creative appreciation to hire some of the nation's most talented artists, whose painstakingly detailed illustrations made farm fields look lush and bountiful.

SAVORY PEAS AND CORN

1/4 cup chopped celery

2 tablespoons chopped onion

2 tablespoons butter or margarine

1/2 teaspoon salt

1/4 teaspoon savory

1/8 teaspoon pepper

1 (17–ounce) can Green Giant sweet peas, drained

1 (12–ounce) can Niblets golden whole kernel corn, drained

1/2 cup dairy sour cream with chives

In a large saucepan, sauté celery and onion in butter until tender. Add remaining ingredients except sour cream; heat through. Stir in sour cream; heat through; do not boil.

Adolf Dehn was an American artist with a wide-ranging regionalistic style. Dehn was born in 1895 in Waterville, Minnesota, and attended the Minneapolis School of Art. His beautiful watercolor scenes of rural farms and farmland are on display in more than a hundred museums, including the Smithsonian. One of the largest collections of Dehn's work is held by the county historical society in Le Sueur, Minnesota, home to Green Giant.

John Ford Clymer, born in 1907, was an American painter and illustrator known for his joyous depictions of nature and the people of the American West. His panoramic watercolors and human-interest subjects appeared in finely crafted picturesque settings, where his visual storytelling abilities brought viewers right onto the farm. His work was featured in many American magazines and museums.

Saving on Wartime Foods

As lush farm produce, nutritious dairy products, and household supplies were needed to support World War II efforts, shortages began to affect just about everyone in America on a daily basis. Minnesota companies rallied to help people manage shortfalls for healthy meal planning. Recipe ideas from clever cookbooks made substitutions interesting, even amusing.

Food rationing was enforced on meats, butter, sugar, fat, and oils, along with many other food products, and those restrictions impacted mealtimes everywhere. Americans were allowed points in ration books that guaranteed each family its fair share of scarce goods.

Your Share

How to prepare appetizing, healthful meals ★ ★ with foods available today ★ ★ ★

Betty Crocker

52 MENUS
226 RECIPES
369 HINTS

On Food Buying, Preparation, Meal Planning and Serving.

MEAT IS SCARCE . . . extend it!

EMERGENCY STEAK

1 pound ground beef

1/2 cup milk

1 cup Wheaties

1 teaspoon salt

1/4 teaspoon pepper

1 tablespoon chopped onion

Mix all ingredients together. Place on broiler pan; pat into T-bone shape, 1 inch thick. Broil 8 to 15 minutes at 500°F. Turn once.

Call **VEGETABLES INTO SERVICE**

Stretch **THE MILK SUPPLY**

Family-oriented poster art was a new trend in wartime communication, with vivid illustrations appearing in cookbooks, magazines, and newspapers. Paper and ink may have been in short supply, but publishers continued to commission noteworthy works of art to promote recipes that saved resources and still tasted like the "good old days."

SCRAPPLE

1 pound lean boneless pork
1 1/2 quarts water
1 1/4 teaspoons salt
2/3 cup cornmeal
pinch pepper
1/8 teaspoon curry and sage, mixed

Cook pork in salted water until tender; shred. Add enough liquid to pork water to make 3 cups stock. Add shredded pork. Bring to a boil. Add cornmeal slowly; cook 20 minutes, stirring constantly. Add pepper and curry and sage. Pour into greased 4x8–inch pan. Chill. Cut into half-inch slices. Fry in bacon drippings or butter until golden brown. Serve with maple syrup.

Persuading the American public to conserve food became a wartime priority, and some of the nation's foremost artists assisted in that endeavor.

Bold words and strong images urged gardeners and cooks to contribute by whatever means they could, and without complaint.

The demand for inspirational art launched a new era in graphic design that quickly evolved into enduring modern styles that would be admired for decades to come.

Victory garden campaigns encouraged people to turn their flower gardens into vegetable patches. Fruits and vegetables were planted on rooftops, in window boxes, and anywhere else families could find space.

The bright pictures and lively activity projected patriotic labor that would supply families with the nutritious foods they needed to stay healthy.

VICTORY PANCAKES

1/2 medium onion

2 medium potatoes

3 carrots

2 cups fresh spinach

1/4 head lettuce

2 eggs, beaten

1 cup sifted flour

1 teaspoon baking powder

1 1/2 teaspoons salt

1/8 teaspoon pepper

Finely chop onion, potatoes, carrots, spinach, and lettuce. Blend in eggs. Sift together flour, baking powder, salt, and pepper; stir into vegetables. Mix well. Drop by spoonfuls into hot fat in skillet. Fry on both sides until golden brown. Serve plain or with cheese sauce.

Crocks, Caves, and Cranks

As home cooks processed and preserved much of Minnesota's garden produce, useful and popular Foley food mills and Red Wing crocks became kitchen necessities—and eventually made their way into homes across the nation.

LAZY WIFE PICKLES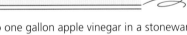

These pickles are so easily made as to be amusing and they are exceptionally delicious in flavor. To a gallon of vinegar add one cup salt and one cup dry mustard. Put this in a stone crock. Take a peck of medium-size cucumbers, wash and dry thoroughly (this is very important), drop cucumbers into the vinegar, and put lid on tight. In the morning the pickles are ready to be eaten. You may add cucumbers from time to time to this same brine so that you may have these delicious pickles all summer. Be sure your cucumbers are dry when dropped into the brine.

CUCUMBER PICKLES

To one gallon apple vinegar in a stoneware jar, add one teacup sugar, one teacup mustard, and one scant teacup salt. Wash and dry medium-size cucumbers. Submerge in stoneware jar, cover with grape leaves and lid. Do not seal. Can be ready for use in a week's time.

Red Wing Union Stoneware Company was a leader in food preservation through its stoneware pots, jars, and churns. The company operated along the Mississippi River, amidst huge clay deposits that were perfect for making the long-lasting stoneware.

By the 1940s, more than one hundred Red Wing tableware designs added decorative charm to everyday meals. A gathering of local artists hand painted every one.

Red Wing cookbooks came sparsely illustrated, but the recipes inside were enlightening and fun to read.

Keep it in Stoneware
The Perfect Preserver of Food Freshness and Purity

In the days before electric blenders and food processors, Foley manufactured hand-operated mills to process food so cooks could make the heavenly sauces and velvety purees called for in modern recipes. Fanciful drawings and confident line work made the tiresome task of mashing and smashing look almost recreational.

The St. Paul company also produced mess kits and other necessities for use in World War II.

CARROT MOUSSE

2 cups cooked carrots	
2 tablespoons butter	
1/4 cup flour	
2 cups whole milk	
1 teaspoon chopped onion	
4 eggs, separated	

Mash carrots through Foley food mill. Make white sauce of butter, flour, milk. Add onion, carrots, beaten egg yolks. Cool. Fold in stiffly beaten egg whites. Turn into buttered loaf pan or ring mold. Place in shallow pan of boiling water. Bake 1 hour at 350°F.

Faribault, Minnesota, is home to huge, awe-inspiring caves, which were used to store beer beginning in the 1850s. When Prohibition nipped beer sales, Felix Frederiksen took over the sandstone caves to make the first American blue cheese. Then, when World War II put constraints on French blue cheese imports, Treasure Cave expanded to become nationally acclaimed for handmade, cave-aged blue cheese.

CREAMY COLESLAW À LA BLUE

1/4 cup sugar	
1 teaspoon salt	
1/3 cup vinegar	
1 cup dairy sour cream	
1 (4–ounce) package Treasure Cave blue cheese, crumbled	
1 medium head cabbage, shredded	

Combine sugar, salt, vinegar, sour cream, and blue cheese. Pour mixture over cabbage and toss lightly. Cover and refrigerate for at least 30 minutes before serving.

New Beginnings

After World War II, the outlook was bright for food industries and the economy was becoming stronger than ever. Families were hopeful about the future, businesses were hiring, and people finally felt secure.

Illustrators responded with buoyant cookbook covers depicting lighthearted scenes of family activities. Minnesota painter Hazel Brewer Wilson used casual brushstrokes in a carefree style that projected the country's return to happiness and togetherness.

SOUR CREAM GINGERBREAD

2 eggs, well beaten
1/2 cup sugar
1/2 cup molasses
1 teaspoon ginger
2/3 teaspoon cinnamon
1 teaspoon baking soda
1/2 teaspoon baking powder
2 cups flour
1/2 teaspoon salt
1 cup sour cream

Cream together eggs, sugar, molasses, ginger, and cinnamon. Add baking soda, baking powder, flour, salt, and sour cream. Bake in a loaf pan in moderate oven about 30 minutes.

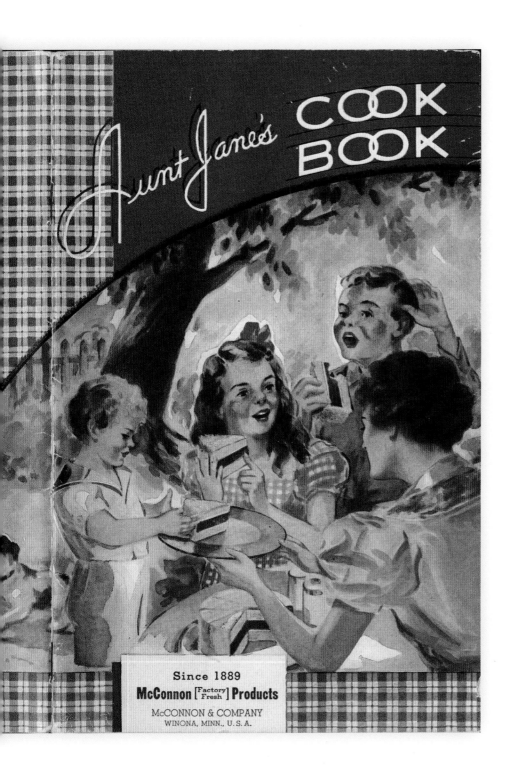

Aunt Jane's COOK BOOK

Since 1889
McConnon [Factory Fresh] Products
McCONNON & COMPANY
WINONA, MINN., U.S.A.

It was happy days in the fifties, and eye-catching figurative art was back in favor. Portrait artists highlighted the decade with cheery faces and joyful activities. Paintings for cookbook covers were full of light and bold in style, and everyone sang for their supper as artfully creative messages promoted local Minneapolis meat markets.

Televisions took a prominent place in living rooms, and up-to-date cookbooks provided inspired recipes to serve modern families—on TV tray tables, of course.

UPSIDE-DOWN HAM LOAF
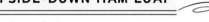

3–4 pineapple rings
1 1/2 pounds ground ham
1 pound ground fresh pork
1 cup bread crumbs
2 eggs
1 1/2 cups milk
1/8 teaspoon pepper
2–3 tablespoons minced onion

Arrange pineapple slices in the bottom of a greased loaf pan. Combine remaining ingredients and pack over pineapple in pan. Bake at 350°F for 1 1/2 hours. Serve hot in slices from the pan or when cool, inverted on a platter.

HAM AND SWEET POTATO ROLL

3/4 pound ground ham	3/4 cup milk
1/2 pound ground pork	pepper
1/2 cup cracker crumbs	2 cups mashed sweet potatoes
1 egg	

Combine all ingredients except potatoes. Spread on waxed paper to half-inch thickness, making a rectangle about 6x10 inches. Spread with seasoned potatoes and roll like a jelly roll. Place in dripping pan and bake 1 1/2 hours at 350°F.

Holiday Greetings from
KIRBY'S MARKET
4803 Nicollet

BARBECUED SHORT RIBS

3 pounds beef short ribs	1 small bottle catsup
1 medium onion, sliced	3 tablespoons Worcestershire
2 tablespoons butter	1 teaspoon mustard
2 tablespoons vinegar	1/2 cup water
2 tablespoons brown sugar	1/2 cup chopped celery
1/4 cup lemon juice	salt and pepper

Brown ribs; transfer to a baking dish. Brown onion in butter. Add remaining ingredients and simmer until slightly thickened, about 30 minutes. Pour sauce over the short ribs, cover, and cook in a slow oven until ribs are tender, about 2 hours. Carrots glazed in the kettle with the ribs are a good accompaniment.

Artful Advertising for Beer

Beer conjured up thoughts of fine art, too, at least in the eyes of talented artists like Norman Rockwell and Les Kouba. Minnesota brewers commissioned ads for celebrating beer in the woods, beer at the lake, beer in the living room, beer in the soup. It all made sense to anyone looking for an excuse to open a nice cold brew.

Norman Rockwell captured American small-town culture with a painting of the local grocer and his anxious card-playing partners. Is he about to put down the winning hand? With easygoing brushstokes, the tense scene still manages to direct the eye to a wooden beer crate and the table set with small bottles of Schmidt's beer.

Joseph Kernan, a go-to artist for beer advertising, took a sportsman's approach for Duluth's Royal Bohemian, Fitger's, and Grain Belt beers. He described his art as featuring the "human side of outdoor sports," and his fresh, open-air paintings were seen on numerous magazine covers and calendars.

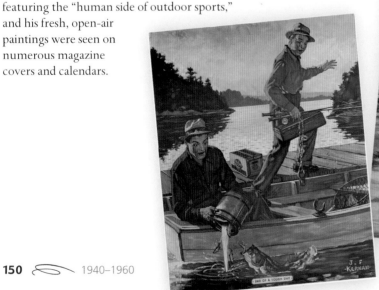

L es Kouba, the dean of Minnesota wildlife artists, celebrated Schmidt's beer through outdoor scenes with the heading "The Brew that Grew with the Great Northwest!" His beer-can art featured the Old West on one side and a modern view on the other—easy entertainment for a beer drinker.

H amm's Brewing took the party indoors, with a group gathered to watch the game on a brand-new television set. The illustrator included women in the mix to convey the smooth and mellow taste of light beer, a product just coming on the market. The formal attire worn by guests at a football viewing party was also appropriate to the time—but wouldn't be for long.

BEER-CHEESE SOUP

4 tablespoons butter

1 carrot, finely chopped

2 ribs celery, finely chopped

1 medium yellow onion, diced

2 cloves garlic, minced

1/4 cup flour

1 cup milk

1 cup half-and-half

1 (16–ounce) bottle beer

1 tablespoon Dijon mustard

2 1/4 cups sharp cheddar cheese, shredded

salt and pepper

Melt butter in a large pot; add carrot, celery, onion, and garlic; sauté until soft. Add flour and cook, stirring, until flour turns golden brown. Pour milk and half-and-half slowly into flour mixture, whisking until combined. Add beer and mustard. Bring to a boil, stirring often. Simmer for 10 minutes, until thick. Remove from heat and whisk in cheese a handful at a time. Add salt and pepper to taste.

Fancy Borders

Fairway Foods takes first prize for fancy border designs on its Christmas recipe and appointment calendars. Swirls and ribbons, curls and cornucopias, fruit and flowers, leaves and vines—all ran around pages in joyful holiday profusion. The family cozied up by the fireplace perfectly fits the description of the 1950s age of contentment.

Fairway Foods Make Happy Homes

STRAND'S STORE

MARINE ON ST. CROIX, MINN.

Fairway Finest Foods
Recipe Appointment Calendar
for 1955

DELICIOUS PEACH CAKE

1 cup Fairway flour
3 tablespoons sugar
2 teaspoons baking powder
1/4 teaspoon salt
3 tablespoons butter
milk
1 can Fairway sliced peaches
sugar and cinnamon

Sift together flour, sugar, baking powder, and salt. Cut in butter. Add enough milk to make a thick, sticky dough. Spread dough into a greased 8x8–inch pan. Arrange peaches closely in rows on top. Sprinkle with sugar and cinnamon. Add dots of butter for richness. Bake in 325°F oven. Serve with whipped cream.

YUMMY CHOCOLATE CAKE

1 1/4 cups sugar
1 2/3 cups Fairway cake flour
1 heaping tablespoon butter
2 ounces baking chocolate
1 egg
1 cup sour milk
1 teaspoon baking soda in water

Sift sugar and flour together; melt butter and chocolate. Mix all ingredients together and bake in a moderate oven.

YUMMY COCOA FROSTING

4 tablespoons butter
6 tablespoons cocoa
5 tablespoons scalded milk
2 cups confectioners' sugar
1/4 teaspoon salt
1 teaspoon vanilla

Melt butter and cocoa over hot water. In a bowl, pour scalded milk over sugar and salt. Stir well. Add vanilla and butter-cocoa mixture. Beat until thick.

Christmas is the most dearly loved of all the holidays. No other day brings so much joy to so many people.

It is the day of peace and good will when families and friends come together in churches and in homes. And the Christmas story that is ever new to starry-eyed children, lives in the memory of grown-ups too as they remember their childhood.

As we wish you the Merriest Christmas you have ever known, we also thank you for your friendship and patronage and hope good health and happiness will always be yours.

OWNER
FAIRWAY FOODS
OPERATED

OLSON'S FOOD MARKET

111 First Street West

CANBY   MINNESOTA

Again it is Christmas . . . the season of good will, good cheer and gratitude for the land in which we live. It is the time that brings happiness and enjoyment to folks like you whose friendship we enjoy.

As families come together and friendships are renewed, we are fortunate that we can gather around the yuletide table loaded down with good things to eat.

It is the children's day . . . the day when their dreams come true. It is the day for grown-ups too . . . when man's faith in mankind is kindled anew.

We are thankful for your friendship and the patronage that we have enjoyed and join with you in the age-old wish of

Peace on Earth
Good Will Toward Men

OWNER
FAIRWAY FOODS
OPERATED

Drive-ins appeared on city streets and rural roads during the 1950s, and illustrations of ice cream cones were emblazoned on menu boards across the nation. As dining styles became ever more casual and convenient, food depictions also changed, with easy-to-read new typefaces and refreshing illustrations.

Few food businesses have survived half a century or more. But for lucky Minnesota ice cream lovers, several companies have remained in the state through thick and thin—and ice and snow.

OLD-FASHIONED FUDGE SUNDAE PIE

24 chocolate Oreo cookies, crushed
1/4 cup melted butter
3 pints vanilla ice cream, softened
1 (12–ounce) jar chocolate fudge ice cream topping
chopped red candied cherries
whipped cream

Blend cookies and butter; press onto bottom and sides of a deep-dish pie pan. Refrigerate for 1 hour. Carefully spread the softened ice cream on the cookie pie crust; top with chocolate fudge; scatter cherries on top. Serve in pie wedges with a dollop of whipped cream.

In 1910 in Maple Plain, Minnesota, Halgren's made deliveries by horse-drawn wagon and milk was poured directly into customers' containers. Butter and ice cream were added in later years, by that time delivered in a Model T truck. The container's patriotic colors of red, white, and blue surrounded a drawing of cool Lake Minnetonka and guaranteed a loyal following.

Starting in 1940, Dairy Queen stores popped up throughout the Midwest, with the company headquarters eventually landing in Minneapolis.

A dollop of soft-serve ice cream in a crunchy cone summoned buyers looking for a take-out treat in a cardboard box. Drawings of the classic Dairy Queen stand brought memories of long waits in long sidewalk lines on long-forgotten summer days.

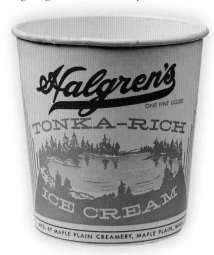

Beginning in 1914 as a small creamery in southeastern Minnesota, Kemps dispensed ice cream to families throughout the Upper Midwest. Northland Milk and Ice Cream company scooped up frosty treats to sell in stores beginning in 1921.

NEAPOLITAN ICE CREAM MILK SHAKE

Mix one pint of Neapolitan ice cream in a mixer or blender with a small amount of milk. Pour into two milk shake glasses, top with a cherry, add a straw.

From Marshall, Minnesota, in 1952, with fourteen gallons of ice cream loaded in an old Dodge van, Marvin Schwan made his first deliveries to local rural families. The Schwan's swirly label, with its immediately recognizable stylized swan, has been with the company since the early days.

N. C. Wyeth and Norman Rockwell

Green Giant had the foresight to hire two famous illustrators of the 1940s and '50s— N. C. Wyeth and Norman Rockwell. Both men crafted noteworthy advertising campaigns over the course of their lifetimes.

A connection was made from the Green Giant farm to the Green Giant table, with expressive and dramatic effect.

CREAMY CORN PUDDING

1 can Green Giant whole kernel corn, drained

1 can Green Giant cream-style corn

1 (8 1/2–ounce) package corn muffin mix

1 cup sour cream

1/4 cup butter or margarine, melted

3 eggs

Heat oven to 375°F. Mix ingredients until blended. Pour into 9x13–inch baking dish coated with cooking spray. Bake 35 to 40 minutes or until golden brown.

One of America's greatest illustrators, N. C. Wyeth described his works as "true, solid American subjects—nothing foreign about them." Wyeth concentrated on personal vantage points so that his art could be understood quickly. He usually painted in subtle hues with an eye to the colors of nature, and he emphasized lively activity. Wyeth cherished the rural American scene, made visible in his harvest painting for Green Giant.

Norman Rockwell was a visual storyteller with a strong sense of connection to everyday people. That focus came through with humor and nostalgia in his entertaining paintings. Bright colors and expressive faces grabbed a reader's attention in an instant.

A full-color print of "Who's having more fun?" could be ordered for ten cents.

Corn came in cans two ways—both on the cob and off the cob. Rockwell's melodramatic images of youngsters eating corn brought a smile to everyone's face.

As farmlands were flourishing, cookbooks concentrated on health and energy with recipes both clever and innovative. Painting styles were changing fast at midcentury. New theatrical approaches to cookbook art lit up covers that called for attention, and colorful billboard-like designs were both daring and dramatic.

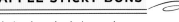

PINEAPPLE STICKY BUNS

1/2 cup drained crushed pineapple

1/2 cup soft butter

1/2 cup packed brown sugar

1/2 cup sunflower meats

1 teaspoon cinnamon

1 can refrigerated buttermilk biscuits

Mix pineapple, butter, sugar, sunflower meats, and cinnamon. Spoon into 10 greased muffin cups. Place biscuits over mixture. Bake 30 minutes at 350°F. Let cool in pans 5 minutes, then invert to release from pans.

MISSOURI CARAMEL DUMPLINGS

1 cup packed brown sugar

3 cups boiling water

3 tablespoons butter, divided

1/2 teaspoon vanilla

1/2 cup granulated sugar

1/2 cup milk

2 teaspoons baking powder

flour

In an ovenproof skillet, boil brown sugar, water, 1 tablespoon butter, and vanilla for 10 minutes. In a medium bowl, mix granulated sugar, remaining 2 tablespoons butter, milk, and baking powder. Add enough flour to make a stiff batter. Drop by tablespoons into the caramel, and bake in the skillet in a moderate oven. Serve hot.

Ceresota Flour Twins

Ceresota Flour operated two flour mills, Ceresota and Hecker, and often featured twins in its artwork. The poster-like quality of this cookbook cover is similar to the postimpressionist style made famous by Henri Toulouse-Lautrec's playbills of 1890s Paris. The images were straightforward in design and graphically engaging, and the pie recipes quite delicious.

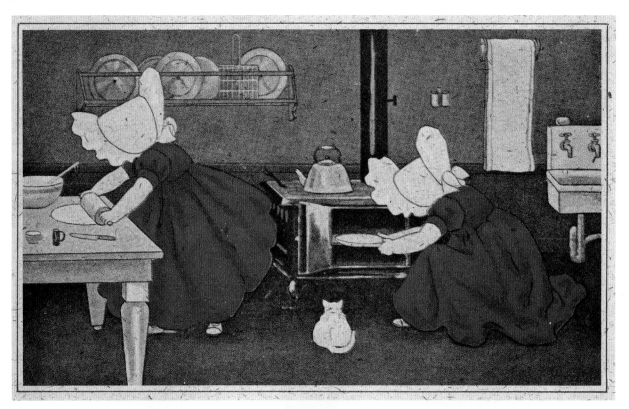

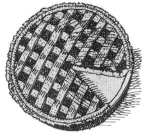

Pen and ink drawings throughout the Ceresota cookbook's pages provided artwork to depict recipes and techniques and added interest for cooks when full-color interiors were not yet practical. Lighthearted, casual line drawings and sketches would become an enticing alternative for illustrating cookbook recipes in years to come.

GREEN APPLE PIE

6 tart green apples

2/3 cup sugar

1/8 teaspoon nutmeg

1/8 teaspoon salt

2 tablespoons dried currants

1/4 teaspoon cinnamon

1/4 teaspoon ginger

1 tablespoon crushed cornflakes

2 pie crusts

1 1/2 tablespoons butter

Peel, core, and cut apples into thin slices. Combine all the dry ingredients and spread over apples; let stand 15 minutes. Place this filling in pie crust. Dot with butter. Dampen edge; put the top crust on; seal and flute. Slash the top crust to let out steam during baking. Bake at 450°F for 10 minutes, then reduce heat to 350°F and bake for about 45 minutes.

CREAMY PEACH PIE

1 can sliced peaches

1 packet plain gelatin

1/4 cup sugar

1 (3–ounce) package cream cheese, softened

2/3 cup evaporated milk, chilled

2 tablespoons lemon juice

1 pie shell, baked and cooled

Drain peaches and save 1/4 cup of syrup. Soften gelatin in peach syrup and melt over hot water. Remove from heat and blend in sugar and cream cheese. Whip the milk in a chilled bowl until thick; add the lemon juice and beat until stiff. Beat in the cheese mixture in 4 additions. Fold in the peaches and pour into pie shell. Chill 3 to 4 hours before serving.

Quick-and-easy appetizer temptations starred in dining rooms of all sorts, nourishing casual solo diners, expanding suburban families, or couples at splendid extended tables.

Old Home Creamery, located in St. Paul, knew how to attract attention with straightforward cartoonlike sketches and simple hand-scribed lettering. Expressive drawings depicted enthusiasm about the fun one could have cooking with cottage cheese.

APPETIZER HAM ROLLS

3/4 cup cottage cheese

1 tablespoon pickle relish, drained

1 tablespoon shredded sharp cheddar cheese

1/2 tablespoon prepared mustard

1 tablespoon mayonnaise

6 thin slices cooked ham

Mix cottage cheese, pickle relish, cheddar cheese, mustard, and mayonnaise. On each slice of ham place 2 tablespoons of mixture, spreading to the edge. Roll up and fasten each slice of ham with a toothpick. Chill, folded side down. Cut in bite-size pieces and insert additional toothpicks for serving.

CHEESY CHILI DIP

2 cups small-curd cottage cheese

1/2 cup grated Parmesan cheese

1/4 cup chili sauce

2 tablespoons chopped parsley

Beat all ingredients together until smooth. Chill.

Dining in Splendor

Weekend breakfast treats

Sat Sun

COTTAGE CLAM DIP

2 cups small-curd cottage cheese

1 medium can minced clams, drained

chives, chopped

salt and pepper to taste

Mix all ingredients together and chill well.

Bountiful Breads from Robin Hood Flour

Famous for more than a century, the Robin Hood brand had come a long way since the days when flour was packaged in wooden barrels. The face of the brand evolved, too: Robin Hood first looked like an Edwardian king, but in 1936, a new design gave him the dashing good looks of Hollywood star Errol Flynn, who portrayed the character in films.

In loose, sketchbook-style illustrations, breads and rolls were given a hard-to-achieve bakery appeal with simple black lines and appealing toasty colors. Despite a light touch, the line drawings still managed to whet the appetite.

A new style of casual illustration opened an intriguing path for future cookbook artists to explore.

APPLE 'N' CHEDDAR MUFFINS

2 cups Robin Hood all-purpose flour

1/3 cup sugar

1 teaspoon baking power

1/2 teaspoon baking soda

1/4 teaspoon salt

1/4 teaspoon cinnamon

1/3 cup grated Parmesan cheese

3/4 cup shredded sharp cheddar cheese, divided

1 egg

1 cup buttermilk

1/4 cup vegetable or canola oil

1 medium tart apple, finely chopped

Preheat oven to 375°F. Grease muffin cups or line with paper liners. Combine flour, sugar, baking powder, baking soda, salt, cinnamon, Parmesan cheese, and 1/2 cup cheddar cheese in large mixing bowl. Whisk egg, buttermilk, oil, and apple together thoroughly in a separate large bowl. Add buttermilk mixture all at once to flour mixture. Stir just until moistened. Fill prepared muffin cups. Sprinkle tops with remaining 1/4 cup cheddar cheese. Bake for 18 to 20 minutes or until a toothpick inserted in center of muffin comes out clean.

Creamette Macaroni

In 1912, James T. Williams invented the first quick-cooking pasta, which he named Creamette. A thinner wall and larger hole were the secrets to the success of his elbow-shaped macaroni. Wanting to pep up a popular everyday product, Creamette put together fun and lively cookbooks with flavorful recipes.

MEXICAN BEEF CASSEROLE

1 pound lean ground beef

3/4 cup chopped green pepper

3/4 cup chopped onion

1 clove garlic, finely chopped

1 (7–ounce) package Creamette elbow macaroni, cooked

2 cups hot water

1 (16–ounce) can tomatoes, cut up

1 (6–ounce) can tomato paste

1 (12–ounce) can whole kernel corn, drained

1/4 cup pitted ripe olives, sliced

1 (8–ounce) can tomato sauce

2 teaspoons chili powder

1 teaspoon oregano leaves

1 teaspoon salt

1/8 teaspoon ground cumin

corn chips, crumbled

1/2 cup shredded cheddar cheese

Preheat oven to 350°F. In large skillet, brown meat; pour off fat. Add green pepper, onion, and garlic; cook and stir until tender. Stir in cooked macaroni, water, tomatoes, tomato paste, corn, and olives. Pour into 3-quart (9x13–inch) shallow baking dish. Stir together tomato sauce and seasonings; combine with macaroni mixture. Bake 25 to 30 minutes or until hot; top with corn chips and cheese. Bake 5 minutes longer or until cheese melts.

MACARONI MEDITERRANEAN

3/4 cup chopped onion

2 tablespoons margarine or butter

1 (7–ounce) package Creamette elbow macaroni, cooked

2 cups cooked chicken or turkey, cubed

1/2 pound hard salami, cubed

1 (10–ounce) package frozen green peas, thawed

1/2 cup pitted ripe olives, sliced

1 1/2 cups milk

1 (10 3/4–ounce) can condensed cream of mushroom, chicken, or celery soup

1 teaspoon salt

1 cup shredded cheddar cheese

Preheat oven to 350°F. In small saucepan, cook onion in margarine until tender. In large bowl, combine all ingredients except cheese; mix well. Turn into greased 3-quart baking dish. Cover; bake 40 minutes. Uncover; top with cheese and bake 5 minutes longer.

SWISS HAM AND NOODLE CASSEROLE

1/2 cup chopped onion

1/4 cup margarine or butter

1 (8–ounce) package Creamette egg noodles, cooked

2 cups cooked ham, cubed

1 (8–ounce) container sour cream, at room temperature

1 cup shredded Swiss cheese

2 eggs, well beaten

2 teaspoons Dijon-style mustard

canned french-fried onions

Preheat oven to 350°F. In a small saucepan, cook onion in margarine until tender. In large bowl, combine all ingredients except french-fried onions; mix well. Turn into greased 1 1/2–quart baking dish. Cover; bake 35 minutes or until hot and bubbly. Uncover; top with french-fried onions. Bake 5 minutes longer.

C ookbook illustrators used playful macaroni art in a decorative pattern as well as in wet noodle typography and necklace design. The fifties-style diner look appealed to readers' taste buds.

Flavors from Europe

As Minnesota's population continued to expand, its newest residents carried with them time-honored recipes and memories of family meals enjoyed in their homelands. Modern-day illustrators connected with these storied traditions by featuring costumed servers proudly carrying dishes laden with back-home fare. Exceptional cooks and genial companionship—a combination that was cause for celebration.

ROAST LOIN OF PORK

1 1/2 tablespoons flour

1 teaspoon salt

1/2 teaspoon sugar

1 teaspoon ground mustard

1/2 teaspoon sage

1/4 teaspoon black pepper

4–5 pound pork loin

TOPPING

1 1/2 cups applesauce

1/2 cup packed brown sugar

1/4 teaspoon cinnamon

1/4 teaspoon ground cloves

Mix together flour, salt, sugar, mustard, sage, and black pepper and rub thoroughly into the loin. Roast uncovered at 325°F for 1 1/2 hours. Combine topping ingredients and spread on roast; continue roasting another hour or until tender.

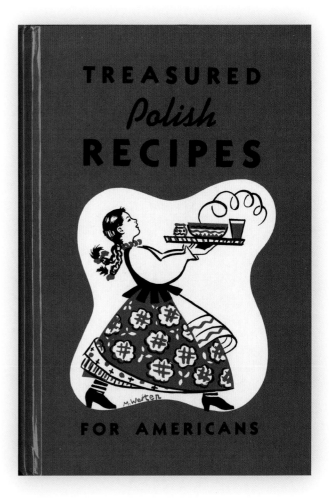

Polish cuisine was influenced by a wide variety of surrounding tastes, including German, Czech, Slovak, Russian, and Italian. *Treasured Polish Recipes for Americans* invited all the neighboring flavors to Minnesota tables.

The cover's illustration of a peasant in traditional dress was drawn by California's Marya Werten, a Polish folk art expert. Interior woodcuts by Stanley Legun, an artist from the Polish community in Northeast Minneapolis, show images of Eastern European table settings.

Scandinavian cookbooks were famous for savory breads and sweet desserts. In fact, the popular smorgasbord was originally a supper buffet of open-faced sandwiches and a seemingly endless variety of tempting pastries. For this early "potluck," everyone contributed to the table. A tray of succulent ham served in period costumes would only heighten anticipation of the sugary cookies to come.

SWEDISH SPRITZ

1 cup butter	
1 cup powdered sugar	
2 1/2–3 cups flour	
3 egg yolks	
1/2 teaspoon salt	
1/2 teaspoon almond flavoring	
1/2 teaspoon vanilla flavoring	

Cream butter and sugar; add remaining ingredients and mix well. Use a cookie press to make various designs, or drop by spoonfuls and make into shapes on a cookie sheet. Decorate with colored sugar and candy. Bake at 350°F about 10 minutes.

NORWEGIAN KRINKLES

3/4 pound butter

1 cup sugar

1 egg

1 teaspoon vanilla

1/4 pound blanched almonds, finely ground

4 cups all-purpose flour

Cream butter and sugar thoroughly. Then add egg, vanilla, nuts, and flour. Roll into 1-inch balls, flatten with fingers on ungreased cookie sheet, and bake 10 minutes at 400°F. Frost with confectioners' sugar and butter frosting. Sprinkle with red and green sugar.

DANISH CONES

1/2 cup butter

1/2 cup sugar

1 cup flour

5 egg whites

Cream butter; add sugar and blend well. Add sifted flour; fold in stiffly beaten egg whites. Spread dough in buttered cake pan and bake in moderate oven until very light brown. Cut into squares while warm and form into cones. Just before serving, fill with whipped cream slightly sweetened and flavored.

By the middle of the twentieth century, American commercial art and design had reduced all things Chinese to the "chopstick/chop suey" typefaces developed a century earlier. A cook looking for a good chop suey recipe—the dish was actually an American invention—had only to look for faux brushstrokes, bamboo stalks, and rice bowls on cookbook covers. Bold graphics may have paid homage to Madame Chiang, but Chun King was a Minnesota dynasty.

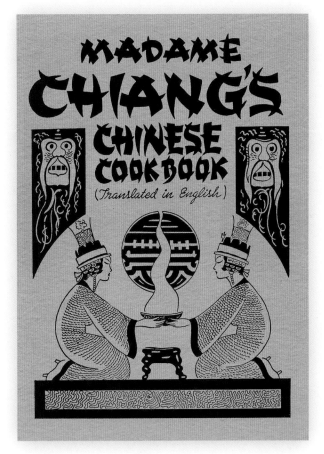

BIRD NEST SOUP

Cut up one dozen Chinese black mushrooms into quarter-inch pieces. Cut one-half can bamboo shoots and six water chestnuts into thin slices. Boil all together in chicken stock about ten minutes, then add two beaten eggs and thinly sliced white chicken meat. Season to taste. This makes a very flavory soup and requires only a few minutes to prepare. Try it the next time you want a good soup in a hurry.

CRAB SALAD ORIENTAL STYLE

Remove cooked crab from shell and tear into small pieces. Add three-quarters cup celery, three-quarters cup bean sprouts, one tablespoon chopped pimiento, one tablespoon minced parsley, and two chopped hard-boiled eggs. Mix with mayonnaise seasoned with one tablespoon Chinese soy sauce. Garnish with quarters of small peeled tomatoes. Serve this with Chinese tea and toasted crackers.

EGG FOO YOUNG

Take a little ham or cooked Chinese pork, two stalks celery, four green onions, one large green pepper, and one-half cup bean sprouts and chop this up fine. Beat six eggs and add the chopped ingredients. Divide this into eight portions and mold just as you would hamburger balls. Place the mixture carefully in a shallow pan and cook over a hot fire, using vegetable oil. When one side is brown, turn over and brown the other side. Make Chinese gravy of one cup chicken broth, one tablespoon each of soy sauce, rice wine, and cornstarch. Heat and pour over the egg foo young and serve with steamed rice.

Founded in Duluth by Jeno Paulucci in the 1940s, Chun King popularized canned oriental foods, contributing delicious ingredients to recipes undertaken by enterprising home cooks. By the 1960s, the company's national reach put it at the forefront of sales in this category.

Those who fondly remember the Minneapolis Nankin Cafe's chicken chow mein can reminisce with a similar recipe from Chun King.

TERIYAKI STICKS

2 pounds beef tenderloin or sirloin, cut into small cubes

2 tablespoons corn oil

1/2 cup Chun King soy sauce

1 cup sherry or rice wine

1/2 cup chopped onion

1/2 teaspoon ground ginger

3 tablespoons sugar

Put 5 or 6 cubes of beef on 12 (6-inch) skewers. Combine all other ingredients and marinate kabobs in sauce for 2 hours. Broil until meat is browned, brushing frequently with sauce.

CHUN KING PLAIN CHOP SUEY

1 pound lean chicken breast

2 tablespoons shortening or cooking oil

1/4 teaspoon salt

2 tablespoons Chun King soy sauce, divided

2 cups sliced or diced celery

1 cup sliced or diced onions

1 can Chun King bean sprouts or chop suey vegetables

1 cup chicken stock

1 tablespoon Chun King brown sauce or beef bouillon

2 tablespoons cornstarch or flour

Cut the chicken into small squares and fry in the shortening or cooking oil, adding salt and 1 tablespoon of the soy sauce. When the chicken is browned and almost done, add the celery, onions, bean sprouts, stock, remaining tablespoon soy sauce, and brown sauce; mix well and cover. When thoroughly cooked, mix cornstarch or flour with water—as for gravy—and add this mixture to the chop suey to thicken it. Then serve piping hot.

Households came together for dinner in front of the TV—maybe to watch a broadcast of Perry Como or Jack Benny on popular variety shows. And, for the first time, complete meals were available in frozen form to families who wanted to dine in modern ways—on TV tray tables or out on the patio. Home cooks copied the style with meat and potato dinners of their own, and leftovers went right into the freezer.

Cookbooks often focused on women's lives, with quaint drawings in buoyant colors. A confident baker in bows and ruffles gazed out from the freezer cookbook with an attitude of humor and friendship.

CRANBERRY-ORANGE RELISH FOR A TURKEY TV DINNER

4 cups cranberries

1 orange

1–2 cups sugar

1/4 cup orange liqueur, if desired

Grind cranberries with the rind and pulp of orange. Mix in sugar to taste, add orange liqueur, and let stand 2 hours. Freeze leftovers.

FROZEN FRUIT SALAD

2 cups sliced strawberries or other berries

12 ounces cream cheese

1/2 cup heavy cream

Mash the berries and combine them with the cheese. Whip the cream and fold it into the mixture. Package in individual paper muffin cups in moisture-proof wrap and freeze at once.

Hot Dishes and Frozen Desserts

Courtesy of Home Service Dept.

MINNEAPOLIS GAS COMPANY

A dreamy illustration from the Minneapolis Gas Company showcased new-age graphics coming into fashion in the late fifties. Art department illustrators were given free rein, and quirky sketches in abstract, expressive designs flew off drawing boards.

Cooking was also becoming a little more adventuresome with the addition of a few "exotic" ingredients to the basic Minnesota hot dish and pasty.

TUNA-NOODLE CASSEROLE

1 (4–ounce) package noodles, cooked

1 (11–ounce) can mushroom soup

1 cup whole milk

1 (7–ounce) can tuna fish, flaked

1 (4–ounce) can sliced mushrooms

3 tablespoons chopped green pepper

1 hard-cooked egg, diced

1/4 cup diced celery

1/2 teaspoon salt

1/2 cup buttered bread crumbs

Combine noodles, mushroom soup, milk, tuna fish, mushrooms, green pepper, hard-cooked egg, celery, and salt. Mix well. Pour into greased casserole. Sprinkle bread crumbs over top and bake at 350°F for 45 minutes. Freeze leftovers for TV dinners.

PORK FOLD-OVERS

1 cup ground cooked pork

1/4 cup milk

1/4 cup catsup

1 tablespoon horseradish

1/2 teaspoon Worcestershire sauce

2 tablespoons lemon juice

salt

2 cups enriched flour

2/3 cup shortening

1/4 cup cold water

Combine pork, milk, catsup, horseradish, Worcestershire sauce, lemon juice, and 1/2 teaspoon salt. Sift flour with 3/4 teaspoon salt. Cut in shortening with pastry blender until mixture resembles coarse crumbs. Add water and mix until dough follows fork around bowl. Toss on lightly floured board and roll thin. Cut in 10 (4x5–inch) rectangles. At one side place 2 tablespoons meat mixture. Fold over and seal edges with fork. Prick top. Bake at 450°F for 10 to 12 minutes.

For a true Iron Range pasty, add cooked chopped onion, rutabaga, carrot, and potato along with the meat.

Nordic Ware

In 1946, Dave and Dotty Dalquist launched the Nordic Ware kitchenware company from the basement of their Minneapolis home. Many of the company's early baking items consisted of old-world ethnic Scandinavian cookware. Joining the lineup of rosette and krumkake irons were grilling tools and cookie presses, and in the 1950s, the Bundt pan was introduced.

When the 1966 Pillsbury Bake-Off contest awarded second place to Ella Rita Helfrich of Texas for her tunnel of fudge cake, demand for Bundt pans suddenly spread worldwide. Nordic Ware employees worked hard to keep up with orders. Still made in Minneapolis, the iconic pans have inspired many intriguing sculptural desserts and are themselves works of art.

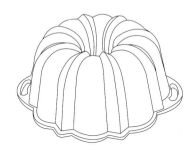

TUNNEL OF FUDGE CAKE

CAKE

1 3/4 cups granulated sugar

1 3/4 cups margarine or butter, softened

6 eggs

2 cups powdered sugar

2 1/4 cups flour

3/4 cup unsweetened cocoa

2 cups chopped walnuts

GLAZE

3/4 cup powdered sugar

1/4 cup unsweetened cocoa

4–6 teaspoons milk

Preheat oven to 350ºF. Grease and flour 12-cup fluted tube cake pan or 10-inch tube pan. In large bowl, combine granulated sugar and margarine; beat until light and fluffy. Add eggs 1 at a time, beating well after each addition. Gradually add 2 cups powdered sugar; blend well. By hand, stir in flour and remaining cake ingredients until well blended. Spoon batter into prepared pan; spread evenly. Bake for 45 to 50 minutes or until top is set and edges are beginning to pull away from sides of pan. Cool upright in pan on wire rack 1 1/2 hours. Invert onto serving plate; cool at least 2 hours.

In small bowl, combine glaze ingredients, adding enough milk for desired drizzling consistency. Spoon over top of cake, allowing some to run down sides. Store tightly covered.

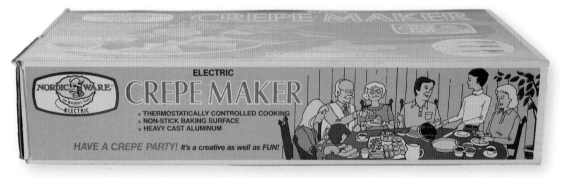

Wearable Flour Sacks

Fabric flour sacks held endless possibilities for homemaker artists. King Midas promoted hundreds of useful articles to wear or perk up the house—all fashioned from flour sacks. Housedresses, school dresses, dressing table skirts, place mats, and rag rugs were only a few suggestions for flour sack fashions.

YOU CAN MAKE HUNDREDS OF USEFUL ARTICLES TO WEAR OR DRESS UP THE HOUSE!

Make yourself this easy-to-wear housedress. Uses 5 50-pound print sacks.

This school dress for your grade-school daughter, uses just three 50-pound King Midas sacks.

Save the scraps from the new outfits you make from King Midas print sacks and braid a gay rag rug like this.

Dressing table skirts are just one of the decorating touches you can add to your home, using King Midas print sacks. All these patterns can be ordered from the address given in the booklet "Thrifty Thrills with Cotton Bags" you can get FREE at your King Midas dealers.

Sew and Save
WHILE YOU ENJOY
BETTER BAKING with KING MIDAS
Just in time for your fall sewing and redecorating, King Midas is now available at your dealers in attractive cotton print sacks.

King Midas ENRICHED FLOUR

King Midas Flour *in colorful cotton print sacks!*

Red and white checks, a popular kitchen design, were used on the cover of *Kitchen Kapers* from the Dairy Council of the Twin Cities.

KITCHEN KAPER CHEESE SAUCE

2 tablespoons butter
2 tablespoons flour
1/4 teaspoon salt
few grains pepper
1 cup milk
3/4 cup grated cheese

In a small saucepan, melt butter and stir in flour, salt, and pepper. Stir in milk. Cook over low heat, stirring continuously until thickened and well cooked. Blend in cheese and continue to stir until cheese is melted and evenly distributed. Serve over cooked vegetables.

King Midas contest winners, called "Baking Queens," were featured in collections of recipes. The Midas touch didn't turn the contestants' recipes into gold—their treasure was recognition for being a good cook.

MILLION-DOLLAR COOKIES

2 cups sifted King Midas flour
1/2 teaspoon salt
1/4 teaspoon baking soda
1/2 cup chopped nuts
1 cup shortening
1/2 cup granulated sugar
1/2 cup firmly packed brown sugar
1 egg
1 teaspoon vanilla

Preheat oven to 350°F. Sift dry ingredients together and mix with nuts. Cream shortening and sugars. Add egg and vanilla. Add dry ingredients and mix well. Form into balls and roll in granulated sugar. Press flat on greased cookie sheet. Bake for 10 to 12 minutes.

CHAPTER 5
1960–1980

*I*n the swinging sixties and seventies, blue jeans, macramé, flower power, and peace-and-love hippies paraded on the fringe of everyday life. During the "me decade" Woodstock and antiwar protests drew crowds and lots of attention. The first man on the moon made Americans proud, the politics of the time challenged people's ideals, and the future carried more than a whiff of unpredictability.

Nevertheless, the fine art of food illustration was soon at its best. Culinary art merged with pop art as vivacious images in recipe books and advertising showcased cutting-edge style in design. Andy Warhol soup cans, Peter Max's bursting colors, and *Star Wars* movie art made the visual world a lot brighter and more imaginative. Comics and cartoons flew off drawing boards with carefree swipes of a pen to entertain and charm cookbook readers.

Home cooking and contemporary entertaining were all the rage as columnists, radio personalities, cartoonists, and even retailers of non-food products published cookbooks. Exotic recipes from around the globe stimulated appetites as the world became smaller. *The Joy of Cooking* was a best seller even as cream of mushroom soup, prepackaged baking products, and onion soup mix went into hot dishes that masqueraded as the latest in fine cuisine. Salad bars and discos awaited diners who wanted to spend less time in the kitchen. Still, as inspiration struck, adept cooks brought home dining to loftier heights.

By the end of the 1970s, the culmination of a century of design had evolved into an elegant simplicity of form, bright rainbow colors, and rich, whimsical abstraction.

Then, suddenly, innovation in food photography brought fine art illustration to an end. With a few exceptions, photography replaced the hand-painted art and creative drawings of the past. Talented photographers fashioned a new approach to still life composition and artistic culinary backgrounds, and food pictures would emerge as a beautiful, but totally different, form of cooking art.

Food enthusiasts had arrived! It was the swinging sixties, and everyone wanted to be a great cook, but they wanted that good food fast. Minnesota companies made certain that mealtime was streamlined with quick pie crust, biscuit, and pancake mixes as well as refrigerated doughs for sweet or savory baked goods. The brand-new Southdale Shopping Center, the first fully enclosed mall, awaited shoppers looking for the latest cooking gadgets. Complicated meal making was on the back burner.

BISCUITS AND GRAVY

Bisquick mix
1 pound uncooked sausage
1/2 cup Wondra flour
3 1/2 cups milk
salt, pepper, and cayenne to taste

Make biscuits according to package directions. Meanwhile, cook sausage in large skillet until browned. Stir in flour; gradually add milk while cooking on medium heat. Cook until gravy is desired thickness. Add seasonings.
Serve hot gravy over biscuits.

Now Betty Crocker gives you a new Ready-to-Bake

HEADSTART ON HOMEMADE

with her whole family of refrigerated foods

Wondra promoted its products in flower power imagery of vivid colors and swirly lines. The quick-mixing flour dissolved easily—no lumps.

Artists painted food illustrations with sixties-style simplicity. True-to-life bronzed crusts and luscious fillings became second nature to those with paintbrush in hand. Grateful cooks found the pie crusts pre-mixed and ready to use, all but guaranteeing an easy and pleasing dessert.

BLUEBERRY PIE

5 cups fresh blueberries

1/2 cup plus 1 tablespoon sugar

2 tablespoons quick-cooking tapioca

1 tablespoon lemon juice

2 unbaked pie crusts

1 tablespoon milk

Heat oven to 400°F. In large bowl, mix blueberries, 1/2 cup sugar, tapioca, and lemon juice. Spoon into crust-lined pan. Top with second crust; seal edge and flute. Cut slits in several places in top crust. Brush top crust with milk; sprinkle with remaining 1 tablespoon sugar. Bake on middle rack, 40 to 45 minutes or until crust is golden brown and filling is bubbly. After 30 minutes of baking, cover crust edge with foil to prevent excessive browning. Cool at least 2 hours before serving.

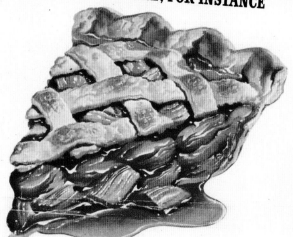

Pamper Papa *with* Homemade Pie
LIKE THIS ONE, FOR INSTANCE

It's easy...quick...with the new
PILLSBURY Pie Crust Mix

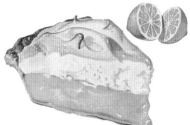

Culinary Art Meets Pop Art

In pop art, artists celebrated commonplace objects of everyday life and elevated popular culture to the level of fine art. It became one of the most recognizable trend-setting styles in years to come. Andy Warhol depicted mass-produced items and readily identifiable objects that were often featured on silkscreen prints.

The contemporary image on the *Minneapolis Star*'s snappy cookbook cover, as well as the trendy flavors featured inside, assured readers that they were truly in modern times.

CRANBERRY SALAD

1 (3–ounce) package raspberry-flavored gelatin

1 cup hot water

1 1/2 cups ground cranberries

1 (8 1/2–ounce) can crushed pineapple and juice

grated rind of 1 orange

1/2 cup sugar

1/2 cup chopped nuts

Dissolve gelatin in hot water. Chill about 15 minutes to thicken. Add remaining ingredients and refrigerate until set.

ESTER'S GLAZED CHICKEN

1 package dry onion soup mix

1 (10–ounce) jar apricot jam

1 (8–ounce) bottle russian-style salad dressing

1 medium to large fryer, in serving-size pieces

Sprinkle onion soup mix in bottom of a 9x13–inch pan. Top with apricot jam, then russian dressing. Stir to mix a little. Rinse chicken pieces and pat dry. Place skin side–down on mixture. Bake in a 350°F oven for 1 hour. Turn chicken and continue baking about 30 minutes or until fork tender.

REST-A-LOT STEW

2 pounds beef stew meat, cubed

1 cup thickly cut carrots

1 cup thickly cubed potatoes

small or large onions, quartered

1 (10–ounce) can cream of mushroom soup

1/2 cup water

salt and pepper to taste

Brown meat, if desired, in small amount of oil. Place with remaining ingredients in medium casserole with tight-fitting lid. Bake in a 275°F oven for 4 to 5 hours.

Helen Federico, who specialized in gouache and acrylic paints, illustrated *Piggy Bank Casseroles* in the pop art style of bold colors and strong outlines.

Taste/the best of Taste
FROM THE MINNEAPOLIS STAR

Newspaper food sections were quick to publish recipe books that satisfied midwestern sensibilities, which at the time often elevated cream of mushroom soup as a star ingredient. Favorite recipes from the weekly "Taste" section of the *Minneapolis Star* were gathered into handy books— no more curling newspaper clippings to save.

Festive Foods

Vibrant recipe books provided by the Minneapolis Gas Company featured colorful illustrations in the pop art style of Peter Max. With his spirited drawings and sketches, uplifting imagery, and artistic diversity, Max influenced American art for generations. His art was often described as the visual counterpart to the Beatles' music.

Modern home cooks would soon be entertaining family and friends in style with recipes from these lively, of-the-moment books. And Minnegasco made certain the directions were calibrated for successful cooking on a gas stove.

CRANBERRY SHRUB

2 quarts cranberry juice
1/2 cup lemon juice
1 quart orange sherbet

Mix cranberry juice and lemon juice; chill, covered. Fill 6–ounce glasses three-quarters full, then add a small dip of sherbet to each.

HA'PENNY SNACKS

1 cup flour
1/2 cup butter
1/4 pound aged cheddar cheese, grated
1/2 teaspoon salt
2 tablespoons dry onion soup mix

Blend together flour and butter. Add remaining ingredients, and when well mixed, form into a roll one-half inch in diameter. Wrap in foil and refrigerate for at least 2 hours. Slice into wafers (three-eighths inch thick). Bake on greased cookie sheets in preheated 350°F oven 10 to 12 minutes. Store in airtight containers.

Columnist Will Jones of the *Minneapolis Tribune* was a big fan of Minnesota food and restaurants. In 1961 he produced a cookbook, *Wild in the Kitchen*, that included his humorous and favorite recipes. Illustrations by Rob Roy Kelly provided zany and quirky commentaries. Kelly, a local graphic artist and instructor, published his own book, *American Wood Type*, on antique and forgotten typefaces, prompting a major typographic revival in the 1970s.

RUBY DEW SALAD

1 red cabbage, shredded
2 or 3 oranges, peeled and diced
honey
lemon juice

Toss the cabbage and oranges together with a dressing made of equal parts honey and lemon juice. Toss salad vigorously while applying the dressing, using only as much as is necessary to coat the ingredients. Let chill in a refrigerator for a couple of hours, and the red cabbage will bleed sufficiently to give a beautiful thin red sauce, which should be spooned over the salad as it is served. The longer this stands, the more it is apt to taste like honeydew melon.

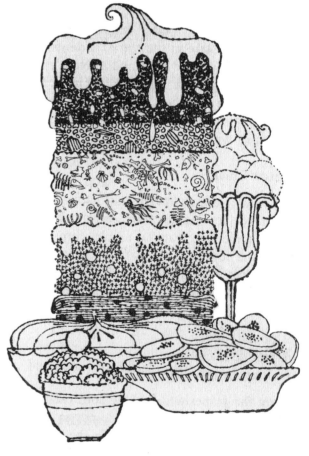

WORKING GIRL'S INSTANT FAKE SWEET-AND-SOUR MEATBALLS

1 egg

1 pound ground round steak

1 bottle chili sauce

1 jar grape, currant, or boysenberry jelly

Mix the egg and meat. Do not season. Form into balls. Mix the chili sauce and jelly together in a saucepan and heat. Drop the meatballs into the sauce and simmer 25 minutes, or longer if you want to play it motherly.

FETTUCINI GUGLIELMO (WITH APOLOGIES TO ALFREDO)

1 (8–ounce) package wide egg noodles

1 package Philadelphia cream cheese

16 tablespoons butter

1/2 teaspoon salt

1/4 teaspoon black pepper

grated cheese (Parmesan, Romano, or Swiss)

While the noodles boil, melt the cream cheese and butter over a low flame, and add 1/2 cup foamy water skimmed bit by bit from the center of the noodle pot. Add salt and pepper to the sauce. Then toss the noodles and the sauce together in a bowl, and serve topped with grated cheese.

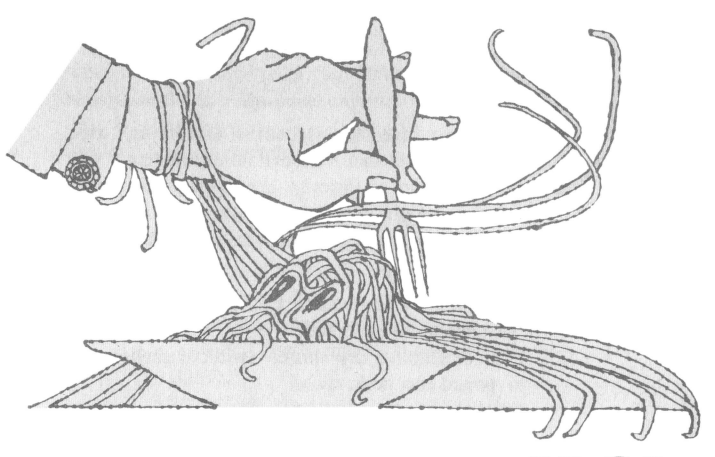

WCCO Radio

Joyce Lamont was a pioneer in broadcasting, and during her five decades at WCCO radio she sent thousands of recipes out over the airwaves to her listeners. In addition to meals made from scratch, her recipes included modern convenience foods such as onion soup mix, muffin mixes, and cream soups that helped cooks wanting to explore fresh flavors and cut cooking time.

FRIED GREEN TOMATOES

3 green tomatoes	3 tablespoons butter
corn muffin mix	salt and pepper

Cut tomatoes into half-inch slices and dip them on both sides in corn muffin mix. In a skillet, melt butter and fry tomatoes on both sides until browned. Sprinkle with salt and pepper and serve immediately.

FOIL-WRAPPED BEEF DINNER

2 pounds beef chuck steak
1 envelope dry onion soup mix
3 carrots, cut into chunks
3 potatoes, peeled and halved
3 ribs celery, quartered
2 tablespoons butter or margarine

Put meat in the center of a piece of heavy-duty aluminum foil, 24 inches long, 18 inches wide. Over the meat, sprinkle onion soup mix. Arrange vegetables on top of the meat. Dot vegetables with butter or margarine. Fold the foil securely around the meat and vegetables, put the package on a baking sheet, and bake for 1 1/2 hours in a 425°F oven.

Celebrating *Joyce Lamont's Favorite Recipes*, pen and ink illustrations beautifully drawn by Patricia A. Canney and enlivened with colorful watercolor washes told the story of simple foods in a setting that included flowers from the garden. Canney's delightful paintings linked life in a small-town café kitchen and her grandma's tailor shop with fond memories of food, flowers, and old-fashioned dresses.

WCCO Radio presents

JOYCE LAMONT'S FAVORITE RECIPES

SCALLOPED POTATOES WITH CHEESE

1 (10 3/4–ounce) can condensed cream of onion soup

1/2 cup milk

1/2 teaspoon salt

1/8 teaspoon pepper

4 cups peeled, thinly sliced potatoes

2 cups shredded cheddar cheese

Preheat oven to 375°F. Make a sauce by combining soup, milk, salt, and pepper. Grease a casserole and arrange alternate layers of potatoes, cheese, and sauce, ending with cheese on top. Bake for 1 hour, covered, then remove cover and bake for another 10 to 15 minutes, until cheese browns slightly.

As the Walt Disney Company's animations boomed in popularity, illustrators everywhere developed their own versions of cartoon art. Humor nearly always won customers, and Schweigert Meat Company of Minneapolis used an engaging cartoon style to its happy advantage. A harried cook or a generous butcher with a tail-wagging dog was sure to entice customers to explore a cookbook filled with economizing sausage recipes.

TAMALE PIE

1 pound Schweigert pork sausage

1 small onion

1 teaspoon chopped garlic

1 (16–ounce) can chopped tomatoes

1 (17–ounce) can whole kernel corn, drained

1 1/2 teaspoons salt

1 teaspoon chili powder, or to taste

1 cup cornmeal

1 cup milk

2 eggs, well beaten

1 cup grated cheddar cheese

Fry sausage in a large skillet, breaking up into small pieces. Add onion with garlic and cook until onion is transparent. Add tomatoes, corn, salt, and chili powder. Blend well and pour into a baking dish. Combine cornmeal, milk, and eggs and spoon over meat mixture. Sprinkle cheese on top. Bake at 350°F for 45 to 50 minutes.

DIXIE SAUSAGE BAKE

1 package Schweigert ham sausage links

1 can sliced apples

1 (16–ounce) can sweet potatoes, drained

1/4 cup packed brown sugar

1/2 teaspoon ground nutmeg

Cut sausage into slices. Brown in skillet. Arrange apples and potatoes in 1 1/2–quart baking dish. Sprinkle brown sugar and nutmeg over apples and potatoes. Arrange browned sausage slices on top. Bake at 350°F for 30 minutes.

WARSAW BAKE

1 medium cabbage, shredded

1 quart sauerkraut, drained

1 package Schweigert Polish sausage

1/2 cup uncooked rice

1 (28–ounce) can chopped tomatoes

1/2 teaspoon salt

In the bottom of a 4-quart casserole, layer half the cabbage. Top with half the sauerkraut. Cut sausage in quarter-inch slices and sprinkle, along with the rice, over sauerkraut. Top with remaining cabbage and sauerkraut. Pour tomatoes over top and sprinkle with salt. Bake at 350°F uncovered for 30 minutes. Cover and bake for 30 to 45 minutes longer or until cabbage is tender.

POOR MAN PÂTÉ

1 package Schweigert Braunschweiger

1 clove garlic, mashed

1 tablespoon chopped parsley, plus more for garnish

1/2 small onion, minced

1 (3 1/8–ounce) can bean dip

2 tablespoons lemon juice

1 (8–ounce) carton dairy sour cream

paprika

Mix first 6 ingredients and pat into molded shape. Refrigerate overnight. Before serving, spread with sour cream. Sprinkle with paprika and garnish with parsley. Serve with crackers.

The LITTLE MEAT COOKBOOK

SCHWEIGERT MEATS

78 ways to make a little meat go a long way

The LITTLE MEAT COOKBOOK
Supplement One

This cookbook was written by women in the Upper Midwest. From the 5,000 recipes received in Schweigert's Budget-Stretcher Contest, 50 of the best appear here. Over a hundred other recipes have been shared via radio. We hope all these recipes help you in your efforts to make a little meat go a long way.

Schweigert Meat Company
2605 Emerson Avenue North, Minneapolis, Minnesota 55411

With acres and acres of parking available, Met Stadium in Bloomington, Minnesota, could host tailgating parties that never wanted to stop. The Twin City Federal cookbook was dedicated to Vikings, Twins, and Kicks fans who "battle wind, rain, sleet, and snow for the fun of eating off rusty, dusty tailgates." Minnesota chef Hank Meadows, host of a daily cooking show on WTCN-TV, contributed recipes to *Tailgate Cooking and Other Gastronomical Horrors.*

TAILGATE BEANS

6 cans lima beans, partially drained

1 bottle catsup

3/4 cup packed brown sugar

2 1/2 teaspoons prepared mustard

1 teaspoon salt

2–3 pounds short ribs, cut and browned well

Mix all ingredients. Bake in bean pot at 350°F until thick and meat is tender (about 1 to 2 hours). May be made ahead and frozen.

Grills were fired up with charcoal lighter from Bloomington-based Holiday stores.

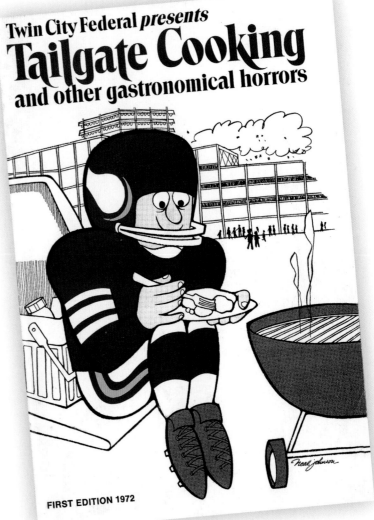

Twin City Federal *presents*

Tailgate Cooking
and other gastronomical horrors

FIRST EDITION 1972

Have FUN... have a...

GLUEK'S
BEER·B·CUE

Simple line drawings in coloring-book style fit the lineup for easy outdoor recipes on game days. Cooks earned a high score on hearty steak and salad lunches for pregame nourishment.

GLUEK'S ROQUEFORT STEAK-CUE

1 thick New York strip steak

1/2 cup Gluek's beer

1/2 cup salad oil

2 tablespoons wine vinegar

1 teaspoon soy sauce

1 clove pressed garlic

1/4 teaspoon thyme

1/2 pound Roquefort or blue cheese

2 tablespoons heavy cream

Marinate steak overnight in mixture of beer, oil, vinegar, soy sauce, garlic, and thyme, turning several times. Blend cheese and cream into thick paste. Broil steak 4 inches from hot coals for 10 minutes each side. Top with creamed cheese and broil 4 minutes more.

ThermoServ, founded in Anoka, Minnesota, in 1956, quickly leapt to national fame with insulated carafes, mugs, tumblers, ice buckets, and serving pieces. Numerous artworks animated the varied products' printed inserts. From anonymous illustrators to well-known local wildlife artist Les Kouba to midcentury modern product designer Georges Briard, there was a style to fit everyone's taste.

HOT GROG

For each serving, heat four tablespoons dark rum, one tablespoon fresh lime juice, one teaspoon brown sugar, four ounces hot water, orange slice, and cinnamon stick.

I n the shell, out of the shell, salted, unsalted, candied, chopped for cookies and breads, crushed into peanut butter—with peanuts, the possibilities are endless. Pile them high in a big bowl next to the potato chips, and this popular pair will get any party off to a happy start.

SALTED PEANUT COOKIES

1 cup butter, softened

1 1/2 cups packed brown sugar

2 eggs

2 teaspoons vanilla

3 cups flour

1/2 teaspoon baking soda

1/2 teaspoon salt

2 cups salted peanuts

Preheat oven to 375°F. Beat together butter, brown sugar, eggs, and vanilla. Blend together flour, baking soda, and salt. Stir into egg mixture; mix in peanuts. Drop by rounded teaspoons on lightly greased baking sheet. Flatten cookies using a fork. Bake 8 to 10 minutes, until golden brown.

FISHER PEANUT BRITTLE
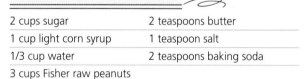

2 cups sugar	2 teaspoons butter
1 cup light corn syrup	1 teaspoon salt
1/3 cup water	2 teaspoons baking soda
3 cups Fisher raw peanuts	

Combine sugar, corn syrup, and water; cook slowly over low heat until sugar dissolves and mixture reaches 240°F, about 30 minutes. Add raw peanuts; cook until mixture reaches 295°F, about 20 to 30 minutes. Do not allow the mixture to boil over. Stir constantly during the following additions. Remove from heat; add butter. Stir until butter has melted completely into sugar. Add salt and baking soda. Stir quickly. Mixture will change color and rise up in the saucepan. Pour mixture evenly onto well-buttered, shallow pan. Work quickly but carefully: mixture is hot. When completely cooled, break into pieces. Store covered.

S am Fisher, a Russian immigrant who served in France during World War I, experimented with salting peanuts in the shell in his St. Paul kitchen. When he and his wife found the secret to tasty roasted nuts, they began selling their popular product throughout the Twin Cities. Soon, the Fisher Peanut Company was delivering these irresistible snacks all across Minnesota and beyond.

Potatoes, a prime crop for Minnesota farmers, were grown all over the state. Potato slices took the plunge into bubbling commercial oil pots on their way to becoming that favorite American snack.

Old Dutch Foods started peeling spuds in 1934, and the company distributed its chips in packaging with the trademarked windmill attached. Pass the dip, please.

Renowned wildlife artist Les Kouba designed the Old Dutch windmill and the Red Owl grocery store logos.

OLD DUTCH SNAPPY DIP

1 cup cottage cheese

1/4 pound Roquefort cheese

2 packages Philadelphia cream cheese

1 clove garlic, minced very fine

1/3 cup chili sauce

1/2 cup mayonnaise

Thoroughly beat together all ingredients until fluffy; refrigerate until thoroughly chilled. Serve with Old Dutch potato chips.

Charles Schulz, the creator of *Peanuts*, featuring Charlie Brown and his band of good-natured cartoon friends, was a Twin Cities native. His simple, clean, minimalist drawings, sarcastic irony, and unflinching emotional honesty connected with readers. *Peanuts* has been seen in 2,600 newspapers in seventy-five countries and read in twenty-one languages.

Schulz's gentle humor appealed to just about everyone, and his cartoons included many food-related commentaries. *The Peanuts Cook Book* included unforgettable icons from the series: Lucy and her lemonade stand, Snoopy kissing Charlie Brown as dinner was delivered. Many recipes appealed to kids who wanted to cook right along with Charlie Brown.

CHARLIE BROWN'S MOTHER'S BUTTERED OVEN POTATOES

4 medium potatoes, peeled

4 tablespoons butter, melted

salt and pepper

Slice potatoes into lengths (like french fries). Soak for 1 hour in ice water. Remove and dry with paper towel. Dip each piece of potato into the melted butter and arrange in a shallow baking pan. Season lightly. Cook in 375°F to 400°F oven until potatoes are brown and tender when poked with a long fork.

If the way to a man's heart is through his stomach, Betty Crocker blazed the trail. Illustrations by Murray Tinkelman animated nearly every page of the book *Foods Men Like*. Pen and ink crosshatching illustrations of roasted chicken or apple pie were highlighted along with baseballers, footballers, doctors, lawyers, and professors preparing to enjoy a big bite. The masterful use of line work in robust and masculine drawings said, "this is man's country—no salad bars here!"

CHICKEN: CRISPY AND OVEN-FRIED

3-pound broiler-fryer chicken, cut up
1/4 cup shortening
1/4 cup butter or margarine
1/2 cup Gold Medal flour
1 teaspoon salt
1 teaspoon paprika
1/4 teaspoon pepper

Heat oven to 425°F. Rinse chicken and pat dry. In oven, melt shortening and butter in 9x13–inch baking pan. Mix flour, salt, paprika, and pepper. Coat chicken pieces thoroughly with the flour mixture. Place chicken skin side–down in melted shortening. Cook uncovered 30 minutes. Turn chicken; cook 30 minutes longer or until thickest pieces are fork tender.

Whimsical Tastes

With notable artists painting in their signature styles, cookbook drawings reached a new level of fun. Illustrations appealed to both art devotees and cooks who appreciated the playful, whimsical drawings. True to the times, the recipes inside followed right along with the informal approach.

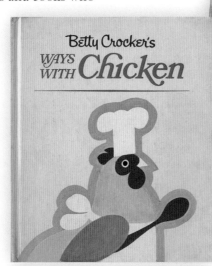

Illustrated by Helen Federico in her characteristic bold, outlined style, *Ways with Chicken* featured simple recipes that made dinner easy to pop on the table.

Crepe paper collage, in which translucent sheets were cut or torn, overlapped, and glued into place, was very popular in the 1960s. Roland Rodegast used the technique to illustrate *Ways with Hamburger* the same year Eric Carle's soon-to-be famous *The Very Hungry Caterpillar* launched the collage look into illustration history.

QUICK CHICKEN À LA KING

1 (10 1/2–ounce) can condensed cream of celery soup

1 cup cut-up cooked chicken

1 tablespoon chopped pimiento

2 tablespoons snipped parsley

salt and pepper

Heat soup. Stir in chicken, pimiento, and parsley; heat through. Season with salt and pepper; serve over toast.

HUNGRY BOY'S CASSEROLE

1 pound ground beef

1 cup sliced celery

1 medium onion, chopped

1/2 cup chopped green pepper

1 clove garlic, minced

1 teaspoon salt

1 (16–ounce) can pork and beans

1 (16–ounce) can lima beans

1 (6–ounce) can tomato paste

In large skillet, cook and stir ground beef, celery, onion, green pepper, garlic, and salt until meat is brown and onion is tender. Drain off fat. Stir in pork and beans, lima beans (with liquid), and tomato paste. Simmer, uncovered, 10 minutes.

innie Weissleder illustrated in spectacular minimalist style, yet the uncomplicated pictures—along with the title, *Show-off Desserts*—conveyed the idea that there were "extra-special" treats inside. With simple lines here and there and dense blocks of color topped with white puffs resembling cream, the message was clear: the finished recipe was going to be a grand addition to the dessert table.

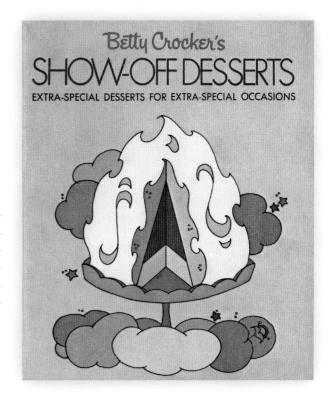

BANANAS FLAMBÉ

1/2 cup butter

2/3 cup packed brown sugar

1 teaspoon cinnamon

4 firm bananas, peeled and cut diagonally into half-inch slices

1/3 cup white rum

1 quart vanilla ice cream

In chafing dish or saucepan, heat butter, sugar, and cinnamon over medium heat, stirring constantly, until mixture is bubbly. Add banana slices; heat through, 2 to 3 minutes. In small saucepan, heat rum until warm; slowly pour over sauce. Do not stir! Ignite immediately and spoon over scoops of ice cream in dessert dishes.

POTS DE CRÈME

4 ounces semisweet chocolate

2 tablespoons sugar

3/4 cup light cream

2 egg yolks, slightly beaten

1/2 teaspoon vanilla

Heat chocolate, sugar, and cream over medium heat, stirring constantly until chocolate is melted and mixture is smooth. Gradually beat mixture into egg yolks. Stir in vanilla. Pour into demitasse cups or other small dessert dishes. Chill.

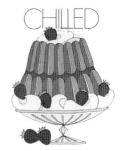

Beginning in 1907, Buzza Company developed its creative spark in Minneapolis by publishing cookbooks, note cards, and paper goods. That great sense of design stayed with the company when it moved to California years later. With fanciful recipes, some by William J. Kaufman, and stunning illustrations by various artists, these lively, vibrant party books inspired celebratory cooks across the nation.

SCALLOPS IN SOY SAUCE

1 1/2 cups soy sauce

4 1/2 tablespoons sugar

3 teaspoons grated fresh ginger

3/4 teaspoon monosodium glutamate (MSG)

1 1/2 pounds bay scallops

Combine soy sauce, sugar, ginger, and monosodium glutamate. Bring sauce to a boil. Add scallops and cook 2 minutes. Place toothpick in scallops to serve.

Harry Ito created illustrations using a wood relief printing technique with pale ink colors that lent *Japanese Dinner Party* a traditional folk art appearance. The book included tips on making party invitations on onionskin paper tied with a ribbon and ornamented with a cherry blossom.

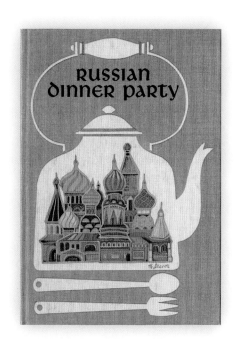

In primitive-style illustrations lacking true dimensional perspective, Howard Jessor portrayed a Russian dinner party filled with foods that would help keep body and soul together through long winter nights. Tables were piled high with folk art serving pieces, and the menu covered everything from vodka aperitifs to dessert.

EGGPLANT CAVIAR

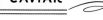

4 tablespoons butter

1 cup chopped onion

1 cup canned tomatoes

1 large eggplant, peeled and diced

1/2 garlic clove

salt, pepper, lemon juice

Heat butter in large skillet; add onion and cook until tender. Add tomatoes, eggplant, and garlic. Cook over low heat, stirring until thick, about 45 to 60 minutes. Remove from heat; add salt, pepper, and lemon juice to taste. Chill. Use as a cracker spread.

BAKED FLOUNDER

8 flounder fillets

salt and pepper

chopped celery, parsley, onion

1/3 cup melted butter

2 tablespoons lemon juice

Sprinkle fish with salt and pepper. Butter a large, shallow baking dish. Cover bottom with chopped celery including leaves, parsley, and onion. Place fish in single layer in baking dish. Combine butter and lemon juice; pour over fish. Bake in a 350°F oven 25 minutes or until fish flakes easily when tested with a fork. Serve with a sour cream sauce.

Amplifying the bravado of the seventies, cookbook style reflected the era's art with high-spirited designs. Bold illustrations from new-age artists were mirrors of quirky and whimsical abstraction.

Illustrated by Linda Badger, *French Flambé Party* was a veritable firestorm of candles and flaming desserts. Highly ornate surface decoration in swirling lines and crosshatching covered every square inch of Badger's illustrations.

STEAK AU POIVRE

coarse ground black pepper

2 porterhouse steaks, 1 1/2 inches thick

1 tablespoon butter

1/2 cup Cognac

Press pepper on both sides of steaks. Heat butter in a large skillet. Add steaks and sear quickly on both sides until cooked to desired degree of doneness. Remove to a serving platter. Add Cognac to skillet; stir to scrape in drippings. Warm and ignite; pour over steaks and serve.

GRILLED TOMATOES

6 small tomatoes

3 tablespoons minced onion or shallots

salt and pepper

1/4 tablespoon thyme

butter

Cut stem and center core from tomatoes. Place cut side–up in a shallow baking pan. Sprinkle with onion, salt, pepper, and thyme; dot with butter. Broil for 10 to 15 minutes, until tomatoes are tender.

FRENCH FLAMBÉ PARTY

With groovy curvilinear line work in the Art Nouveau Revival style, *Creole Mardi Gras Party*'s illustrations danced right off the pages. Artist Leslie Pierce engaged readers in glamorous scenes saturated with color. The book was entertainment waiting to happen, and if there wasn't yet an event on the calendar, just looking through the pages could be a party in itself.

LOUISIANA SWEET POTATO PECAN PIE

9-inch unbaked pie shell

1/3 cup granulated sugar

1/3 cup packed light brown sugar

1/4 teaspoon salt

3/4 teaspoon ground ginger

3/4 teaspoon ground cinnamon

1/2 teaspoon ground nutmeg

1 cup mashed sweet potatoes

2 eggs, well beaten

3/4 cup hot milk

1/2 cup packed light brown sugar

1/4 cup butter softened

3/4 cup pecans, chopped medium

Line a 9-inch pie plate with pastry. Combine white and brown sugars, salt, and spices in mixing bowl. Blend in mashed sweet potatoes. Beat in eggs. Stir in hot milk. Pour into unbaked pie shell. Bake 25 minutes in a 375°F oven. Blend 1/2 cup brown sugar with butter and pecans. Sprinkle over partially baked pie. Continue baking 30 minutes or until filling is firm in the center. Serve hot or cold, with whipped cream.

The joyfully painted *Pie and Pastry Cookbook* from Betty Crocker was a wonder of artistic exuberance. Colors danced across the cover, swirled around piles of fruit, and came to rest on a table filled with alluring pastries and vegetables.

The cover art was provided by Wilson McLean, who illustrated for music albums, sports magazines, children's books, movie posters, and book jackets, among many other commissions. Interior drawings were provided by Bill Goldsmith, a freelance illustrator and graphic novelist.

PIES! PIES! PIES!

That's what this book is all about—pies. The full range is covered—

• Appetizers • Main Dishes • Desserts

Traditional pie and pastry recipes are included, along with up-to-date methods and tips for using convenience foods—a boon for the novice and the experienced homemaker alike.

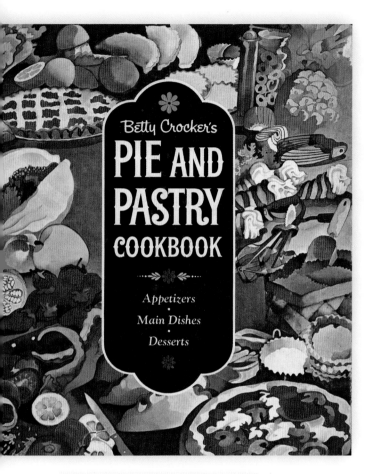

GRASSHOPPER PIE

1 1/2 cups chocolate wafer crumbs

1/4 cup melted butter

32 large marshmallows

1/2 cup milk

1/4 cup crème de menthe

3 tablespoons crème de cocoa

1 1/2 cups chilled whipping cream

few drops green food coloring, if desired

grated chocolate

Preheat oven to 350°F. Mix crumbs and butter. Press mixture firmly and evenly on bottom and sides of pie pan. Bake for 10 minutes. Cool. In saucepan, heat marshmallows and milk over medium heat, stirring constantly, just until marshmallows melt. Chill until thickened; blend in liqueurs. In chilled bowl, beat cream until stiff. Fold whipping cream into marshmallow mixture; fold in food coloring. Pour into crust. Sprinkle grated chocolate over top. Chill several hours, until set.

VANILLA SOUR CREAM PIE

8-inch baked graham cracker crust

1 cup dairy sour cream

1 cup milk

1 (3 1/2–ounce) package vanilla instant pudding mix

Prepare crust. Beat sour cream and milk with rotary beater until smooth. Blend in pudding mix until mixture is smooth and slightly thickened. Pour into crust. Chill at least 1 hour or until set. If desired, serve with sweetened whipped cream. Top with sliced strawberries or peaches.

For chocolate sour cream pie, follow recipe above except substitute 1 (4 1/2–ounce) package chocolate instant pudding for the vanilla instant pudding.

Our book of one hundred years of illustration celebrates Minnesota food artistry in countless ways. From simple black and white etchings to intricate full-color oil paintings, appreciation of the delightful art in cookbooks, on product labels, and for national advertising has been memorialized on these pages.

Food photography has become the art of the future, and beautiful pictures will come from photo studios instead of from easels and drawing boards. The talents and expertise of a totally different kind of artist will inspire new appreciation.

Yet, for those who value the fine art of Minnesota cooking, talented artists will continue to paint beautiful pictures and devise stunning illustrations for the region's food companies.

Hopefully, the art and recipes gathered here will energize cooks of the future and excite artistic generations to follow.

In *Tempt Me*, we have preserved some of the fine art from our cooking history and a taste of the period foods from Minnesota's past. We may never know the subtle influence those trends have had on our lives, but we are grateful for the artistic visions they represent.

Wouldn't one taste good — right now!

Milky Way
"When you crave good candy"

Franklin Clarence Mars learned the art of candy making from his mother and by the age of nineteen was running a wholesale candy firm in Minneapolis. In 1923 Frank Mars created the Milky Way candy bar, and by 1929 it was the number-one-selling candy bar in the world.

Index

Italicized page numbers indicate an illustration.

Index

Credits

Images in this book are shown by the generosity of the following companies, societies, and individuals. It was an honor to peek into company archives and witness the visual history of Minnesota's products and promotions. Individual collectors in the area also graciously allowed us into their homes and lent us items from their personal archives. Thank you all for sharing your treasures. (Images not noted are from the authors' collection.)

ANDERSON HORTICULTURAL LIBRARY

From the Anderson Horticultural Library, University of Minnesota, Chanhassen, Minnesota: cover, apples; 24–25, Jewell Nursery; 27, May's tomato, Cumberland Cucumber; 28, Northrup, King & Co.; 29, Brazilian Melon Fruit, *Seeds for Garden–Farm–Lawn*, Jewell Nursery raspberries; 37, Northrup King & Co.; 40, Jewell Nursery apples; 41, Farmer Seed and Nursery Co., Minnetonka apples; 60–61, three Farmer Seed and Nursery Co.; 71, five seed packets; 72, Northrup King & Co., Farmer Seed & Nursery Co. bean box; 142–43, two handbooks

GENERAL MILLS

Courtesy of the General Mills Archives: 15, The World is Ours, Washburn-Crosby Co.–Merchant Millers; 48, *A Little Book for A Little Cook* cover; 133 Bisquick ad; 139, Green Giant wreath, *War Work: A Daybook for the Home;* 157, four Norman Rockwell paintings; 180, Wondra, Headstart on Homemade; 181, Pillsbury Pie Crust ad and three pies; 182, *Piggy Bank Casseroles*

HENNEPIN HISTORY MUSEUM

cover and 64, *Sunday Magazine;* 141, *War Work: The Second Year*

HORMEL FOODS

SPAM and HORMEL are trademarks of Hormel Foods, LLC and used with permission from Hormel Foods Corporation. 118, Hormel Ham ad; 119, SPAM ad

MINNESOTA HISTORICAL SOCIETY

12, Gardner Mill; 13, Columbia Mill, New Prague Flouring Mill Co.; 22–23, four *What to Eat* cover images; 33, Cream of Wheat; 39, four Occident Flour paintings; 65, *Win-the-War Cookery;* 67, *War Time Recipes;* 74–75 , two Occident Flour ads; 84, WPA campfire; 97, Pillsbury ad; 104–5, three Pillsbury ads; 116, WPA campfire; 129, Cream of Rye; 130–31, two *The Farmer's Wife* magazines; 134–135, five Pillsbury Pancake Flour ads; 155, *Charming Desserts;* 158, two *Pick Sunflower Recipes* images, *Bakery Art;* 171, Nankin

MINNESOTA STATE FAIR ARCHIVES

69, Milton Dairy butter sculpture

NORDIC WARE ARCHIVES

174–75, Bundt pan illustration, Electric Crepe Maker, Cookie King, Aluminum Griddle

OLD DUTCH FOODS, INC.

195, Old Dutch logo

PEARSON'S CANDY CO.

103, candy wrappers

BEVERLY BAJUS

165, Robin Hood Flour *Let's Bake*

JOHN BREYFOGLE

30, Home Brand Rolled Oats; 42, Blue Bird Coffee; 43, Our Family Cocoa; 56, Foster's Allspice; 59, McMurray's Country Club; 80, Seal of Minnesota; 128, McConnon ginger

MARGARET CARPENTER

59, Mischief cinnamon

CHUCK DONLEY

195, Red Owl

BILL HEFNIDER

150, Fitger's Beer

VICKE HEGEDUS

Abdallah's candy box, 103

LINDA HERBERGER LAMSKI

42, Moccasin Coffee; 58, Behnke & Co. cayenne pepper, Trillium black pepper, Thistle cream tartar, Land O' Lakes allspice, Fullarton's sage, Home Brand cinnamon, Old Faithful cloves; 59, Fort Snelling sweet marjoram, City of Lakes sage, Minnehaha nutmeg, Hillcrest turmeric, Gopher ginger

RON KELSEY

80, all feed sacks except Seal of Minnesota. Thanks, Ron, for showing your collection at the Minnesota State Fair.

STEVE KETCHAM

vi, Blue Earth City Rollermills; 42, Table King Coffee; 43, Wak-em Up Coffee, Wampum Coffee, Arrow Coffee; 69, Season's Greetings from Milton Dairy Co.; 77, Zumbro Valley Sugar Corn; 78, St. Bonifacius Canning Co.; 82, Ginger Ale; 83, Sarsaparilla, Sweet Apple Cider, Cream Soda; 213 Towle's Log Cabin Maple Syrup

ALLAN KLEIN

i, *The Farmer Country Kitchen Cook Book;* 2, coffee pot from *The Farmer Country Kitchen Cook Book*

TIM PICHE

150, Royal Bohemian

BILL RUDAHL

150, Schmidt Beer

GLEN WIESSNER

103, two National Candy Company boxes

PHOTOGRAPHY

Thank you to Jim Castle for professional photography of most of the artifacts in this book. His attention to detail made the book's objects come to life.

OCCASIONAL ART

Pen and ink artwork used throughout this book came from 1907's *Daniel Webster Flour Cook Book,* published by New Ulm's Eagle Roller Mills and illustrated by Krieg.

SCANNING

Thanks to Steven Kaiser and Shoua Thao for their numerous hours dedicated to scanning the hundreds of images in this book.

COLOPHON

This book was designed within blocks of the Pillsbury A Mill in Minneapolis. Fonts include Spectrum, Frutiger, Jolly, Rosalinda, and Milanette Ornaments.

SUGGESTED READING

- Falk, Peter Hastings. *Who Was Who in American Art.* Madison, CT: Sound View Press, 1985.

- Heimann, Jim. *May I Take Your Order? American Menu Design 1920–1960.* San Francisco, CA: Chronicle Books, 1998.

- Reed, Walter. *The Illustrator in America: 1860–2000.* New York, NY: The Society of Illustrators, 2001.

- Seddon, Tony. *Twentieth Century Design: A Decade-By-Decade Exploration of Graphic Style.* Blue Ash, OH: Quid Publishing, 2014.

- Simon, Howard. *500 Years of Illustration.* Mineola, NY: Dover Publications, Inc., 2011.

"They've just heard the St. Regis serves Ry-Krisp"

Oh, what a beautiful evenin'... with a girl who can't say "no" to delicious Ry-Krisp at the St. Regis! Smart girl! She knows a "hit" bread when she tastes it. Ry-Krisp is whole rye—crisp baked into dimpled brown wafers —with a flavor as tantalizing as the latest tunes. For a late snack—a just-us-two supper — peddle over to the St. Regis and call for Ry-Krisp.

Ry-Krisp crackers were baked in Minneapolis beginning in 1899. Originally, Scandinavians were the biggest customers, but over the years the worthy crisps won universal enthusiasm for holding up delectable mixtures of cracker spreads.

SALMON SPREAD

8 ounces cream cheese, softened

1/2 cup sour cream

1 tablespoon lemon juice

1 tablespoon dill, minced

1 teaspoon horseradish

6 ounces smoked salmon, chopped

salt and pepper

Mix cream cheese with sour cream. Add all other ingredients. Mix well.

One more cup of coffee
with a delicious piece of cake?